D0389572

Advance Praise for Thomas George and *Blitzed*

"Quarterback is the most popular position in football, and football the most popular sport in America. In *Blitzed*, Thomas George takes readers on a fascinating inside journey of the high-stakes risks and rewards of that job, and how far teams will go to ride a young gunslinger to success. A terrific insider's view from a long-time football insider himself."

—Mitch Albom, *New York Times* bestselling author and sports columnist for the *Detroit Free Press*

"The biggest mystery in modern football is not what team will finally dethrone the Patriots for NFL supremacy, but rather which hotshot college quarterback will become a professional star. Thomas George rationally and methodically puts a microscope on this conundrum, from what happens when a coach realizes his bonus baby doesn't have the goods ("Devastating," Dick Vermeil calls that feeling) to enlightening chapter and verse on the Eagles' pursuit of new great quarterback hope Carson Wentz. I'm glad George doesn't advance a theorem that will guarantee success for a young quarterback because, as he lays out, there simply isn't one."

—Peter King, editor in chief, *The Monday Morning Quarterback*

"*Blitzed* by Thomas George is a through, complete, and riveting study of the challenge faced by teams trying to find and develop a franchise quarterback. As one who has lived it, I can tell you that *Blitzed* is a 'must-read' for every NFL fan."

—Bill Polian, former general manager of the Indianapolis Colts, NFL analyst with ESPN, and Hall of Fame executive

"A franchise quarterback is the NFL's most important asset, and *Blitzed* is the most important work on this subject. Thomas George delves into the subject of franchise quarterbacks, trying to explain the riddle that baffles and bewilders the worst teams, and rewards and stabilizes the best ones. It is educating, enlightening, and highly enjoyable."

—Adam Schefter, ESPN NFL Insider

"I've known Thomas George for a long time and have always respected the quality of his work. He puts years of experience and expertise covering the NFL to excellent use in *Blitzed*. With particular focus on Carson Wentz, Jared Goff, and Dak Prescott, George dissects the trickiest task in sports—finding and developing the franchise quarterback. How do you know when a quarterback has that "it" factor? Thomas knows."

—Jim Thomas, NFL writer, *St. Louis Post-Dispatch*

"Thomas George has written one of the most important books about the NFL in years. *Blitzed* is a provocative first-hand look at how NFL teams thrust very young men into the most difficult position in professional sports and demand they succeed—now. I could not put this book down."

—Sal Paolantonio, National Correspondent, ESPN

"Thomas George has spent thirty-five years seeking answers to what makes some NFL quarterbacks great while others fail. In *Blitzed: Why NFL Teams Gamble On Starting Rookie Quarterbacks*, he uses his wealth of experience and lifetime of NFL contacts to explore what has become the central issue of successful team building in the NFL. Why are more rookie quarterbacks being handed the ball and why do so few succeed? What determines success or failure? Thomas George set out to find the answers and succeeded like Tom Brady. By the time you finish *Blitzed* you'll understand why more and more teams risk the future on rookie quarterbacks and why all but a handful are doomed from the start."

—Ron Borges, writer for *Boston Herald* and author of
Present at the Creation: My Life in the NFL and the Rise of America's Game

"Thomas George knows the ins and outs of the NFL and, in particular, NFL quarterbacking. He dives into the age-old issue of finding a franchise quarterback in an insightful way. George's interviews with coaches who have found and failed to find that star quarterback provide deep analysis of the biggest challenge for pro football teams. And his examination of the flops is especially enlightening."

—Barry Wilner, pro football writer, Associated Press

"Ever wonder why some early-round quarterbacks thrive and others fail? Thomas George goes behind the scenes to give you the answers from the coaches and decision-makers whose livelihoods depend on making the right choice at the game's most important position."

—Alex Marvez, writer for *Sporting News* and host of SiriusXM NFL Radio

BLITZED

BLITZED

WHY NFL TEAMS GAMBLE ON STARTING ROOKIE QUARTERBACKS

THOMAS GEORGE

FOREWORD BY WARREN MOON
AFTERWORD BY TONY DUNGY

**SPORTS
PUBLISHING**

Sports Publishing books may be purchased in bulk at special discounts for sales promotion, corporate gifts, fund-raising, or educational purposes. Special editions can also be created to specifications. For details, contact the Special Sales Department, Sports Publishing, 307 West 36th Street, 11th Floor, New York, NY 10018 or sportspubbooks@skyhorsepublishing.com.

Sports Publishing® is a registered trademark of Skyhorse Publishing, Inc.®, a Delaware corporation.

Visit our website at www.sportspubbooks.com.

10 9 8 7 6 5 4 3 2 1

Library of Congress Cataloging-in-Publication Data is available on file.

Cover design by Brian Peterson
Cover photo credit: AP Images

Acknowledgment of Pro-Football-Reference.com for use of its extensive research and statistics.

Print ISBN: 978-1-68358-107-9
Ebook ISBN: 978-1-68358-108-6

Printed in the United States of America

To my family near and far, and to all those who appreciate this incredible game's enchanting tapestry.

TABLE OF CONTENTS

FOREWORD BY WARREN MOON

Nobody wants a good quarterback. Every team and every coach in the NFL wants a great quarterback—someone they can build a franchise around. As a Hall of Fame quarterback, many people have asked me, "What makes a 'franchise quarterback' so special?" In my opinion, what makes that type of player different is that he gives you the opportunity to win *every* week, no matter your opponent. A franchise quarterback provides an air of confidence that's not only noticeable in the locker room, but is present within the building, stadium, and organization. Nothing compares to having your fan base rally around the guy who is behind center, knowing that he's the right player to lead the team and franchise.

The perception around the NFL is that if you don't have a great quarterback, then you're probably not going to have a very competitive football team—especially due to the way the rules have changed in recent years. Today, quarterbacks are protected in the pocket and defensive backs cannot be as physical with receivers, so that it is more of a pitch and catch type of game for the offense. As a result, the quarterback position dominates the game, making having a "franchise" quarterback even more important.

Transitioning to the NFL from college, rookie quarterbacks quickly realize that professional football is a completely different ball game. In college, you're typically not playing against exceptionally talented teams every week and there might only be two or three players on opposing teams that have the talent to play in the National Football League. Then, suddenly, upon entering the NFL, you're playing against 52 guys who were the very best in college, and have the tenacity to win. As a rookie, you have to adjust to the fact that there are no glaring weaknesses in anybody's game. You're playing against *the best* cover guys and pass rushers in football, the game moves *a lot* faster, and windows to make throws close quickly.

What's tougher than playing against the best guys, though, is playing *with* some of the worst. The worst teams get the highest draft picks, so that means the highest-drafted quarterback will usually go to a bad football team. This usually puts the player in a situation where he doesn't have any pieces around him to make his adjustment easier. More is put on his shoulders, which is the situation you see with a lot of today's young quarterbacks in the NFL. If they can make it through that transitional period without losing all their confidence and getting too beat up (a classic example of this is the Texans and David Carr), they have a chance of success if the team continues to build around them—and that's assuming that the team keeps moving forward without taking any steps back. Another critical issue among young quarterbacks is when teams change offensive schemes or have a revolving door of coaches, which can stunt the growth of any quarterback, something that many fans of the game fail to realize.

I had four different offensive coordinators and two different head coaches in my first four seasons, which made things difficult.

NFL fans, often holding extremely high expectations, desire consistent success from their team and quarterback. One of the things I am most excited about with *Blitzed* is that fans will have the opportunity to gain a deeper appreciation of what it means to be a successful quarterback in the NFL. Being a quarterback, especially a rookie QB, requires a lot more than what fans see on the field. By reading the information in this book, you get to learn not only from quarterbacks themselves, but from general management, coaches, owners, and scouts on what they're looking for when they draft a player they hope is a franchise quarterback. Of course, much of what you're looking for is the physical attributes, but there are so many intangible characteristics that go into making a great quarterback that you can't always judge by looking at a guy on the field. What's inside of him? What's in his heart? What is his work ethic like? Is he prepared to handle adversity—not only on the field, but off the field in his personal life?

Most of all, I hope that thinking about these types of questions will help readers realize the immense amount of pressure that comes with drafting a quarterback and trying to develop them into an All-Pro. There is a lot of research, thought, and hard work that goes into the decision for an organization to draft a quarterback and, even then, nothing is certain. Remember, success for a young quarterback is not as simple as being talented. Achieving success as a quarterback is a combination of being put in the right situation, getting an opportunity with the right coaches, system, and teammates, and, finally, leading your team to victory.

INTRODUCTION:
THE QUEST, THE GAMBLE

Why do NFL teams gamble on starting rookie quarterbacks?

Because they crave franchise quarterbacks.

The search can be frustrating. Exasperating.

"This is the guy that is the difference-maker," Hall of Fame and Super Bowl XLI winning coach Tony Dungy said. "There are 32 NFL teams. Unfortunately, there are not 32 franchise quarterbacks. There are always going to be teams that need one. Always teams that are looking. The trend nowadays is to draft them, play them, see if they can rise to that franchise level—or move on and try it again. A young one sets you up for the next ten to fifteen years. If you've got one, you're going places."

And if you don't?

"You can feel deprived," Super Bowl XXXVII winning coach Jon Gruden said. "You can feel desperate. There is a sense of urgency. So, you see teams draft them and start them instantly to try to fill that void. We've seen teams shoot way up in the draft with big, costly trades to go get the franchise quarterback they have identified. We've seen teams fall into franchise quarterbacks with late-round picks. It all begins to shake out on who's right and who's wrong. But, to be honest with you, I don't know if it's fair to call much of it a gamble. If you're picking at the top of the draft, you've got a problem—you probably don't have one. And the top-quality quarterback is usually at the top of the draft.

"If you don't have one, where are you going to get 'em? Free agency? What quarterback is usually worth a damn in free agency? A trade? Who trades a quarterback worth a damn? You basically get them as rookies in the draft. You are hoping they will become a franchise quarterback, a long-term winning quarterback, a Super Bowl–winning quarterback. I was accused of never getting (drafting/acquiring) a great quarterback when I coached. Some years, it's just pure luck who is available and who is not available in the draft. I mean, how much of a genius do you have to be to pick Andrew Luck when he's coming out? Or Peyton Manning? I know Bill Parcells in Miami took [offensive tackle] Jake Long at No. 1 overall [in the 2008 draft] ahead of [current Atlanta Falcons quarterback] Matt Ryan. How do you think Miami would look today with Matt Ryan?[1]

"So it's a gamble, but it's also the luck of the draw. And then it's just mistakes made letting people slip through the cracks. They said [Seattle Seahawks quarterback] Russell Wilson was too short. [Dallas Cowboys quarterback] Dak Prescott was too zone-read oriented. [Oakland Raiders quarterback] Derek Carr was a kid with nothing lacking, but teams were spooked by how it turned out for his brother [2002 No. 1 overall pick David Carr]. [Hall of Fame quarterback] Joe Montana's arm was not strong

---

1. In 2012, the Dolphins drafted Ryan Tannehill with the 8th overall pick, hoping he would be their franchise quarterback. Questions remain.

enough. These guys were passed over, later with deep regret. That's the crapshoot."

* * *

Why do NFL teams gamble on starting rookie quarterbacks?

Sometimes, the rookie quarterbacks are deemed instantly better than the team's veteran alternative. Sometimes, NFL head coaches feel pressure from owners and fans to toss rookies in quickly—even before the staff feels they are ready. Sometimes, NFL head coaches do it as a job-saving act, in fear of being fired and a new coach reaping the rookie's possible benefits. Sometimes, salary cap structures expedite the rapid insertion.

Since 2011, of the twenty-five rookie quarterbacks taken in the first two rounds of the NFL draft, only five have failed to be their team's primary starter in their rookie season.[2] For the last nine consecutive NFL seasons, at least one rookie quarterback has started his team's season opener. Consider that the prior longest such streak was only four straight seasons (1968–71).

In the 2014 NFL season, Minnesota Vikings quarterback Teddy Bridgewater started 12 games, broke 91 Vikings rookie passing records, and was named the Pepsi NFL Rookie of the Year. In the 2015 NFL season, Jameis Winston and Marcus Mariota were drafted 1-2 and have already become staples with the Tampa Bay Buccaneers and Tennessee Titans, respectively.

---

2. Colin Kaepernick (49ers, 2011), Jake Locker (Titans, 2011), Brock Osweiler (Broncos, 2012), Jimmy Garoppolo (Patriots, 2014), and Christian Hackenberg (Jets, 2016).

In the 2016 season, rookie quarterbacks Carson Wentz, Dak Prescott, Jacoby Brissett, and Cody Kessler combined for a 7–2 record with 6 touchdown passes and 0 interceptions in the first three NFL weekends. Prescott started every game in '16, leading Dallas to a 13–3 record and into the playoffs.

In the 2017 NFL Draft, three teams selected quarterbacks among the top 12 picks and each team traded up from its lower draft position to make that happen, led by the Chicago Bears catch of Mitchell Trubisky at No. 2.

* * *

All rookie quarterbacks struggle. Most never reach franchise status. But when it clicks, it resonates.

The Super Bowl is the target. To reach it, to win it, franchise quarterbacks are routinely required.

Add potential Hall of Fame inductees Peyton Manning, Drew Brees, Tom Brady, Aaron Rodgers, Ben Roethlisberger, and Eli Manning, and 38 of the 51 (74.5 percent) Super Bowl–winning quarterbacks are Hall of Famers. Of the 51 Super Bowl–winning quarterbacks, only two own losing career records: Joe Namath (62–63–4) and Doug Williams (38–42–1).[3]

NFL franchises spend countless hours and resources identifying quarterbacks who showcase thick skin as much as talent. Often what one team sees in that trait, another team misses. What one talent evaluator concludes, another one across the league has an opposite view. Increasingly, NFL teams are focusing on a quarterback's toughness, hardness factors.

---

3. Jim Plunkett had a .500 career record, at 72–72.

"I read a lot about the military," Super Bowl XXXIV winning coach Dick Vermeil said. "In the military, they cannot predict who will be the best under pressure. But they wonder, who will be the 'medal guy?' The military is spending a lot of money trying to identify in advance who is that guy among them that is most excellent under pressure. Well, with NFL quarterbacks, there's a little something to that. Sometimes the closer you get to that No. 1 pick for your hoped franchise quarterback, the gamble increases. But Dak Prescott was drafted in the fourth round. That is not a gamble, period, at that draft slot. Jared Goff to the LA Rams for that steep of a cost to the Rams? To me, that is a huge gamble!

"Sometimes you just don't see it and you miss on a quarterback like Dak. Other times you wonder a bit, like I do with Goff. And sometimes you just know. I was coaching a preseason game in the seventies and remember going out for warm-ups. We were playing the Baltimore Colts. They had Bert Jones at quarterback. First time I saw him, I told my coaches, 'Holy Mackerel!' I had never seen anyone throw the ball the way he threw the ball. It was like that with John Elway, too. Just know this: It's the most devastating thing in football when you draft a guy and you walk off the practice field thinking, 'Oh my God.' And you realize he is nowhere as good as you had hoped. That does happen, you know. Just devastating. I prefer you play the rookie quarterback right away. Play them now. You need to know."

But, even so, it is hard to know.

The leadership, the communication skills. The intelligence, the DNA, the mentality and processing skills. The toughness. The personality and how it meshes in the locker room. Can he handle being the franchise guy? Can he handle being "The Show?" The idol worship?

The correct answers are hardly a cinch.

Will he ever master handling sophisticated NFL defenses? He must be able to decipher how current NFL defenses stroll and wander before the snap, rarely making pre-snap commitments to specific alignments. Can he deal with hybrid defensive players who now pass rush as much as they drop into coverage? Can he sidestep a rush, dance, and still throw accurately? Can he keep his eyes downfield instead of fretting over being crushed? Can he dial it into tight, closing pass defense windows?

And while doing all this, can he manage his offense, his huddle, his peers, and get his team out of bad plays and into good ones with audibles?

Aaron Rodgers said this about one of the most incredible plays of the 2016 season. It was his third-down, off-balance, 36-yard completion to tight end Jared Cook inches from the sideline. It led to a Green Bay Packers playoff-winning field goal in the final seconds at Dallas. "I'm confident anytime I'm out there, game on the line or not, but we've made those throws before in practice," Rodgers said. "It's a matter of trusting your muscle memory and your training, and thinking about a positive picture when you break the huddle and executing it right away."

That is how you want your franchise quarterback to play and to think.

Every team, every coach wants that approach and mindset.

Sometimes, even when teams get it, they find it tricky to artfully coach.

"I also think it's not gambling when you draft and play a rookie quarterback," two-time Super Bowl–winning head coach Mike Shanahan said. "You have to get that quarterback situation set up for the present and the future. It's probably the most poorly evaluated position in sports. Everyone knows a championship team separates itself from the pack by having a good quarterback. And once you get him, you have to be very specific about what he can and can't do. Very few of them can do it all."

These factors make the high-pick, franchise quarterback drafting experience a potential disaster. It fosters varied philosophies on not only how to select, but also how to effectively groom rookie quarterbacks.

The intensity of making the proper decisions and the debate on the approach for developing rookie quarterbacks has been debated in pro football for more than half a century. Prime examples are the NFL drafts of 1948 and 1956, and what happened in those quarterbacks' careers.

In the 1948 NFL Draft, the Washington Redskins used their No. 1 pick on quarterback/halfback/defensive back Harry Gilmer. Hall of Fame Quarterback Bobby Layne was selected No. 3 by the Chicago Bears. Hall of Fame quarterback Y. A. Tittle was taken No. 6 by the Detroit Lions. Layne sat his rookie season behind Sid Luckman and Johnny Lujack. Tittle opted for the Baltimore Colts of the then All American Football Conference and, as a rookie, passed for 16 touchdowns. He turned a 2–11–1 team from the season prior into a 7–7 team, made the playoffs, and won the AAFC Rookie of the Year. Thus, the Redskins took Gilmer over two eventual Hall of Fame quarterbacks.

In the 1956 draft, safety Gary Glick was the No. 1 pick by the Pittsburgh Steelers. Quarterback Earl Morrall was No. 2 by the San Francisco 49ers, where as a rookie he was a backup to Tittle (Tittle had moved to the 49ers by then). Morrall later became a key figure in the Miami Dolphins' 1973 undefeated season. And who was the No. 200 pick of the 1956 draft? It was Green Bay

Packers Hall of Fame quarterback Bart Starr. Starr was a backup to Tobin Rote his rookie season, and did not become the Packers starter until 1959, which was also head coach Vince Lombardi's first year with the Packers. Gary Click or Bart Starr? The answer is so simple now.

But in the moment, nailing the winning choice can be onerous.

The latest example of an overlooked, over analyzed, botched rookie quarterback projection is Dak Prescott. In the 2016 NFL Draft, seven quarterbacks were selected before him. But his rookie season was so good that the Cowboys already consider him their franchise quarterback. He enjoyed a stout offensive line in 2016. He enjoyed a robust running game. His passing accuracy, too, was rare. He won the AP Offensive Rookie of the Year award and was selected to the Pro Bowl. He was a fourth-round pick, No. 135 overall. It was Tom Brady–like: the sixth-round player, the No. 199 pick in 2000. The quarterback who fooled them all en route to five Super Bowl rings.

"Tom [Brady] works very hard and prepares well," said Bill Belickick, the New England Patriots head coach and five-time Super Bowl winner. "He's very diligent in his preparation. It's not an up and down thing. It's consistent every week in terms of learning the defense, learning their schemes and their players. Just getting our game plan so he knows what we're doing and how we're doing it, he's able to put it all together better than any player that I've ever coached. Putting that together in just a couple of seconds of time, he has to process it once he gets the calls and to the line of scrimmage. I think his preparation allows him to in part do that. He's a great role model for all of us. Any player and any coach. All of us."

But Brady didn't start as a rookie. In fact, he only appeared in one game in 2000, completing one pass on three attempts. Belichick emphasizes that Brady was groomed in his 2000 rookie season while he sat behind veteran quarterback (and former No. 1 overall pick) Drew Bledsoe.

"Every team essentially has the same opportunity based on the current NFL rules in place for that season," Belichick said. "We have to maximize our opportunities, whatever those are, to develop young players at this and every position. Player development does not end in the rookie year. It is an evolving process that encompasses several years. As someone who did not play his rookie year, Tom Brady would be one good example of this."

Gruden and Vermeil describe some rookie quarterbacks who were drafted highly but struggled mightily—David Carr, Kyle Boller, Joey Harrington, Tim Couch, Akili Smith, Heath Shuler, Ryan Leaf, and many others—as a mixed bag who blew their chances or were "victims." Each NFL team may enjoy similar opportunities, but not all teach, coordinate, or cultivate rookie quarterbacks effectively.

"We have over the years chewed them up and spit them out and in many instances still do," Los Angeles Chargers head coach Anthony Lynn said. "We've killed the confidence of a few of them. There is no telling how many rookie quarterbacks we've ruined. Everybody is not a Peyton Manning. For some, it just takes time. Personally, I prefer the situation where you have a veteran winning quarterback and the luxury of sitting the rookie the first year so that he can watch and learn. That's the perfect situation. That's the way it used to commonly be, but it's harder and harder to come by."

The pressure to win, the economics, the head coach's job (in)security, and the stunning success of some rookie quarterbacks can make the gamble enticing.

Or, again, ruinous.

Few young quarterbacks can match Blaine Gabbert's trials, his odyssey.

In 2011, Gabbert was drafted in the first round, No. 10 overall, by the Jacksonville Jaguars. In 2011, his head coaches were Jack Del Rio and Mel Tucker; in 2012, it was Mike Mularkey; in 2013, it was Gus Bradley; in 2014, he moved on to San Francisco to play for Jim Harbaugh; in 2015, it was Jim Tomsula; in 2016, it was Chip Kelly.

For the 2017 season, Gabbert, now twenty-seven years old and with the Arizona Cardinals, will have his eighth head coach (Bruce Arians) in seven seasons.

That is a myriad of coaches, offensive systems, and change. It is a potential mind-blowing experience for a young quarterback.

"The supporting cast and the system make a big difference for rookie quarterbacks," Gruden said. "Some of these teams have changed coaches and coordinators like they change shorts."

Some NFL teams, especially the Cleveland Browns and the New York Jets, have spun in circles for decades trying to identify a franchise quarterback.

Hall of Fame safety Ronnie Lott said: "A lot of times, these scouts and coaches don't know what they are looking at. They make the same mistakes. They pick the wrong guys. And then these quarterbacks just don't know what they don't know. It's about making crucial decisions at crucial times in the game. That's hard."

Consider that the Browns three times since 2000 have used pick No. 22 of the first round to select a quarterback: Brady Quinn (2007), Brandon Weeden (2012), and Johnny Manziel (2014). None stuck.

Longtime NFL offensive whiz Chan Gailey, now retired, used to often say that everyone is called at different times to do different things in the NFL. Everyone must be included, Gailey insists. "That's what makes a team."

Most of the NFL will shoot right back: No franchise quarterback, no NFL nirvana.

NFL head coaches know that the lack of a franchise quarterback often is a genesis for their firings.

Seventy-five NFL head coaches who were with their teams for four or fewer years were fired or forced to resign from 1998 through 2016. Of those 75 coaches, 22 were fired after two seasons and 11 were fired after one season. Those 75 coaches worked with only 18 Pro Bowl quarterbacks. Nine of those 18 quarterbacks made the Pro Bowl only once in their careers. Twenty-four of these coaches started rookie quarterbacks in eight or more games.

NFL head coaches seek time to tutor rookie quarterbacks. In many instances, they are denied. Ownership, fans, and critics often demand microwave results in a show-me-now, pressurized league.

No franchise quarterback, no NFL nirvana.

The rookie quarterback must be surrounded in the quarterback room by coaches and peers who can positively influence his study habits. NFL teams are pondering for future choices what works best and what innovative approaches—including virtual reality exercises—can be incorporated.

"It's difficult to win without a good quarterback," San Francisco 49ers head coach Kyle Shanahan said. "Look at the history of the NFL. Teams that don't have one of those guys usually struggle to be there at the end of the year unless they have one of the top defenses in Super Bowl history or NFL history. Everyone knows that. You need a quarterback to be consistently competitive. That's what everybody is looking for, coaches and personnel people. It's usually where it starts."

The 2016 NFL Draft and the regular season that followed provided a premier example. The Los Angeles Rams (Jared Goff at No. 1) and the Philadelphia Eagles (Carson Wentz at No. 2) bolted to the top of the draft via pricey trades in order to select these potential franchise quarterbacks. Once obtained, each team employed opposite answers to this recurring riddle . . .

Start him?

Or . . .

Sit him?

Chapter 1
START HIM?

The Philadelphia Eagles reside in the NFC East, a conference long known for featuring heroic quarterback play and Super Bowl champions. But only the Eagles among the NFC East group of the Dallas Cowboys (five times), New York Giants (four times), and Washington Redskins (three times) have failed to win a Super Bowl.

After the 2015 season, the Eagles realized that Dallas was still banking on veteran quarterback Tony Romo, the Giants still enjoyed the mature hand of Eli Manning and Washington was enjoying the emergence of Kirk Cousins.

The Eagles' owner, Jeffrey Lurie, was not happy with his quarterback quandary.

Lurie bought the Eagles in 1994. He paid $185 million for them to then-owner Norman Braman, who had lost his zest for ownership, unhappy with free agency and soaring player salaries and unmoved in his belief that the rocketing cost of franchise quarterbacks helped split a division among most locker rooms that was unmanageable.

It took Lurie five years to find a franchise quarterback when Donovan McNabb was nabbed with the No. 2 overall pick in the 1999 draft. It took six years after that for the Eagles to reach Super Bowl XXXIX, a 24–21 loss to the New England Patriots.

Lurie has not had a whiff of the Super Bowl since that game in 2005.

Nor a franchise quarterback.

He fired head coach Andy Reid after the 2012 season, courted college coaching whiz Chip Kelly from Oregon, and fetched veteran quarterback (and former No. 1 draft pick) Sam Bradford among a series of futile moves in recent years. In November 2015, he began hearing whispers about this wunderkind quarterback from tiny North Dakota State. Lurie heard chatter about the 2016 draft presenting two highly projected franchise quarterbacks.

So, in December 2015, Lurie set out on an old mission in a new way.

"I define a franchise quarterback as someone who has the physical talent, the mental leadership qualities, and mental toughness to be a consistently winning quarterback that puts you in contention to win a championship," Lurie said. "He has to have that 'it' factor. The single most important trait is the mental fortitude to handle the challenges that face a young quarterback. He has to be a smart quarterback—in today's NFL, quarterbacks have to routinely make intricate decisions in 2.5 seconds or less.

"We looked at the crop of future 2017 quarterbacks and we thought the 2016 group showed us we'd better act now. Was there a franchise quarterback we could move up in the draft to get? Was this the year to get what we have been looking for, searching for such a long, long time?"

Those early whispers from November 2015 came from Eagles personnel executive Tom Donahue. He told Lurie there was this small-conference quarterback from North Dakota State who looked bright and talented. Who looked interesting. His name was Carson Wentz. Cal quarterback Jared Goff was also beginning to create buzz. Lurie listened. Lurie was intrigued.

A month later, Lurie fired Kelly as his head coach. In January 2016, he replaced him with Doug Pederson, in part because of Pederson's offensive, quarterbacking acumen. And Lurie made sure that Pederson had other equipped offensive-minded coaches around him, including offensive coordinator Frank Reich and quarterback coach John DeFilippo.

Then Lurie hit the road with his new head coach, general manager Howie Roseman, and a contingent of Eagles coaches and staff, all on a franchise quarterback expedition.

"I first saw Carson at the Senior Bowl in 2016," Lurie said. "Our scouts were there. Then we all went on this quarterbacking tour in late March where we met the quarterbacks in their environments. We visited Carson in North Dakota. We visited Goff at Cal. We went to Paxton Lynch at Memphis and to Kevin Hogan at Stanford. We saw some others. It wasn't just to say hello. I wanted to spend time with them. We had a strategy in place."

It was find the right guy.

The right rookie quarterback.

A franchise quarterback.

Then to move up to the top of the draft from their No. 13 spot in the first round and swipe him.

Decidedly, mercilessly, take a bolder shot at solving their lingering franchise quarterback enigma.

* * *

Wentz wowed the Eagles at the Senior Bowl. He wowed them on their tour visit. He wowed them at the combine. He continued to wow them when he visited Philadelphia afterward.

It was his size. His arm. His intelligence. His command. His personality. His skill.

Wentz thinks he understands the connection, now saying about his new town, his new team, his new home: "They love hard work and they love winning. That's the biggest thing, and I'm the same way. I hate to lose. If you're not working hard, I don't really tolerate it either. So, I think it's a great fit for me."

Wentz sure looked like the missing puzzle piece.

Lurie said his pre-draft work showed him that Wentz was remarkable in his poise, confidence, and humility. He considered Wentz a quick thinker. Lurie describes Wentz's confidence as strong but not arrogant, "an impressive air for what he was then, a twenty-three-year-old." He said Wentz was "hungry" and that the quarterback's pre-draft trip to Philadelphia was a reconfirmation of the Eagles' earlier assessments.

"We were quite focused on Carson and we decided we wanted the No. 1 pick for the 2016 draft," Lurie said. "But we were at No. 13. How would we get there? The first move was getting from 13 to No. 8, and I give Howie credit for creating a deal with the Miami Dolphins to achieve that.[1] We learned the St. Louis Rams were very aggressive in getting to No. 1, and our intel said they wanted Goff. We got to No. 2 and took our chances that the Rams were not bluffing."

---

1. On March 9, 2016, the Eagles traded Byron Maxwell, Kiko Alonso, and the No. 13 overall pick to the Miami Dolphins for their No. 8 overall pick in the draft.

The Eagles traded three top 100 picks in the 2016 draft: their first-round pick in 2017 and a second-round pick in 2018 to the Cleveland Browns for the No. 2 draft slot. A lofty price they appreciated when the Rams, indeed, selected Goff at No. 1 and Wentz fell to them at No. 2.

"It was a relief," Lurie said. "Our plan came to fruition. I was just very excited for us. It was a ton of research. A study of quarterbacks. We believe we found a young man who has all the ingredients of a franchise quarterback—and, yet, we still don't know. I've been at this long enough to know it really takes a few years to know. It takes every ingredient possible, particularly staying healthy and improving. Surviving the mental part of that first year is the hardest and most valuable."

The Eagles faced that itchy riddle . . .

Start him?

Or sit him?

The plan was for Wentz to sit and learn behind Sam Bradford. McNabb had done that as a rookie behind Doug Pederson, thus further defining Pederson's Philadelphia connection. Lurie and Pederson agreed that Wentz would be best served to watch, wait, and be groomed behind Bradford.

But that began to steadily and then quickly change.

From the earliest camp workouts, Wentz rapidly ascended. Reich, in an early June camp interview, raved about how Wentz's "aptitude was off the charts."

Lurie expounded: "Both Frank [Reich] and John [DeFilippo] began telling me very early in the process that this guy is ready if we need him, that if he had to play he could play. They described it as almost 'unprecedented.'"

That readiness factor was cemented by this one: the Minnesota Vikings had lost starting quarterback Teddy Bridgewater to injury and called the Eagles in early September requesting a trade for Bradford.

"We were going to play Sam, we had signed him to a two-year contract before the season, but we also knew he was a tradeable asset. And this was a way to get our assets back from the trade to move to No. 2. We determined it was the best of both worlds—not in the short term, but the long term. Carson gets to play right now. We get draft picks back.

"Do you play your rookie franchise quarterback right away, or do you sit him? There is no perfect way. It is a matter of your strategy in how you develop quarterbacks. What are his strengths and weaknesses? Where does he come from and from what system? Peyton Manning and Troy Aikman started as rookies and took their lumps; they had the mental toughness to not only survive it but grow from it. We felt the same way about Carson."

Wentz had orchestrated a pro-style offense at North Dakota State and was granted tremendous liberty in audibles and in his decision-making based on his progressions and analysis of defensive tactics.

The Eagles were aligning Wentz with other rookie quarterbacks in NFL history who were resilient and surprisingly effective as rookie starters.

Among the most recent were Jameis Winston with the Tampa Bay Buccaneers in 2015, who threw 22 touchdown passes as a rookie. Andrew Luck in 2012 with the Indianapolis Colts helped push his team into the playoffs as a rookie, throwing for 4,374 yards. Russell Wilson in 2012 (26 touchdown passes, 10 interceptions) led the Seattle Seahawks into the playoffs. Matt Ryan in 2008 produced a rookie season that included his first NFL pass—62 yards for a touchdown—one of 15 more touch-down passes that season and nearly 3,500 passing yards. Ben Roethlisberger in 2004 won 13 straight games as a rookie with the Pittsburgh Steelers and helped ignite his team into the AFC Championship game.

For most rookie quarterbacks—even potential franchise quarterbacks—starting an entire season can be a pit worth avoiding; especially if a proven, valuable veteran can lead.

Pederson countered, as Wentz took the starting role: "Everyone feels like this kid is ready to go and we drafted him to take on the reigns—it's something we're prepared to do."

The Eagles saw a nimble mind, a big arm, maturity beyond his years, and let Wentz sling it.

In fact, Pederson literally made the call a week before the Philadelphia 2016 season opener against the Cleveland Browns at home.

Wentz took the actual phone call that he would be the team's starter while lying on the ground geese hunting in New Jersey. Lurie was certain the Eagles were making the right call well before that.

"I invited all of the quarterbacks during training camp to my box for a concert that was in our stadium, Sam, Carson, and Chase Daniel," Lurie said. "Carson didn't want to come. He graciously declined. He said he had done nothing in the NFL as yet and did not want his teammates to think he deserved such a privilege. He said he believed the veteran players wanted to see young quarterbacks working extra hard, not being treated in exceptional ways in the owner's box. I respected his feelings. I was not surprised. I told him the hopes I had in him. I told him there would be a time it would be OK. This was not only the type of quarterback, but the type of person we were turning to as our franchise quarterback."

* * *

For the franchise, the move was a quick step toward the future. In the minds of some veteran Eagles, however, it was a white flag tossed for the 2016 season. *A rookie quarterback is a rookie quarterback*, they thought. *There are clearly reasons why a rookie quarterback had not started an Eagles season opener since 1939*, they mused. *He does nothing for our playoff hopes this year*, they grumbled.

"There were a lot of attitudes about a lot of what was happening, but it was up to Carson to make his teammates believers," Eagles safety Malcolm Jenkins said. "He set out to do that. He wasn't selected No. 2 overall for no reason."

The Eagles players before Wentz's NFL debut were impressed with his mind and his mobility.

Tight end Zach Ertz said: "Throughout the spring and summer he showed a lot of good things. The way he can move helps us expand the playbook. That can be a good thing."

From his first pass against the Browns on the bright afternoon of September 11, 2016, at Lincoln Financial Field, Wentz made that his business. He threw for 278 yards and two touchdowns in leading the Eagles to a 29–10 victory. He did it while his quarterback counterpart, Robert Griffin III, started for the Browns. Griffin struggled mildly, going 12-for-26 with 190 yards and an interception before being injured late in the game.

Wentz, the quarterback the Browns had passed on, the one they let the Eagles draft with their original pick, the quarterback Browns executive Paul DePodesta had described as not being "a top 20 NFL quarterback," had snuffed them in his NFL debut.

"You know, a lot of stuff gets said during the draft process and it continues throughout the season and your career," Wentz said in a private moment after the game. "But I focus on just getting better and being prepared. I know I have a lot I can build on from this game. Really, though, I'm just finding my way."

Though Browns management were doubters, their players left that debut offering glowing analysis of Wentz, including then Browns receiver Terrelle Pryor, who said, "That kid's going to be a baller," and cornerback Joe Haden, who said, "He was more advanced than I expected him to be."

Eagles defensive tackle Fletcher Cox described Wentz after his debut: "I think he played with a lot of energy. I said earlier in the week there is just something about that kid. I think he's going to be real special in terms of how he handles things and plays with poise. He just lived in the moment this week."

Pederson added: "It's not surprising, because we've been around him so long now and just know the maturity level that he has and the things I was trying to get across to the fans, to the media: This is who he is. This is his DNA."

Wentz led the Eagles to a 3–0 start. During that winning streak, he threw 5 touchdown passes and no interceptions and produced a 103.8 passer rating. He became the first player in NFL history with 100-plus passing attempts, 60-plus completions, 5-plus touchdowns, and zero interceptions in his first three starts. Consider that Peyton Manning threw 8 interceptions in his first three career starts and Troy Aikman threw 6.[2]

---

2. In addition to Manning and Aikman, Terry Bradshaw and Fran Tarkenton each threw 5 interceptions in their first three starts, while Joe Montana and John Elway threw 3.

That 3–0 start was capped by a victory over Pittsburgh, a Wentz victory that induced Eagles veteran tight end Brent Celek to proclaim: "I told coach [Pederson], being ten years in, this kid is inspiring me. He's adding youth to my game just by the way he's acting, being in the huddle, taking command, it's beyond impressive. It's great. We have to keep it going. I'm excited with how he's playing and he's elevating everyone's play by the way he's handling it."

Praise for Wentz surfaced among opposing coaches.

"Carson Wentz has the tools you are looking for in a franchise quarterback," said an NFL head coach whose team played against Wentz during his rookie season. "He's 6-foot-5, so you like that. I would be a little concerned about his accuracy on the deep ball as the season progressed. That part of his game deteriorated. But for a rookie performance, it was pretty encouraging for Philadelphia."

Eagles offensive tackle Lane Johnson was sold after that first game: "He is a big, strong guy. He can handle it. He is a big boy. I am proud of him for the way he handled it. There was a lot on his plate today. He took the team by the reins. It's his team now."

The Eagles coaches and players were also impressed with Wentz's cool demeanor. Wentz said he was on fire inside but his exterior presented none of that.

"Believe it or not, Carson was calm before the game," then Eagles running back Kenjon Barner said. "You guys don't get to see him on a daily basis like we do, but he is a confident guy. He believes in his ability and God has truly blessed him. What he did today was display to the world what he displays to us on a daily basis."

As with most rookies, Wentz struggled as the season progressed. His mechanics and decision making were flawed. His offensive line was jumbled. His receivers displayed shortcomings.

After dropping four of their next five games, the Eagles improved their record to 5–4 when they beat the eventual NFC champion Atlanta Falcons in Week 10. They then lost five straight games.

Wentz pointed at himself.

"I made my share of mistakes and there were many things I could have executed much better last season," he said in review of his rookie year. "Sometimes you are just sort of learning as you go and you can't make up for not having the experience. But I think we have all built a strong foundation together."

Pederson does not believe he overloaded Wentz in his rookie year.

"No, because you've got to know Carson Wentz. You've got to know his chemistry, how he's built, and how he's wired."

The Eagles finished 2016 with a 7–9 record, winning their final two games against NFC East division rivals the New York Giants and Dallas Cowboys. Both of those teams were playoff bound. Wentz winning divisional games to end the season was an encouraging moment for Pederson and Lurie. For Lurie, the season ended just like it started.

"We were all pretty excited after the Cleveland game, even though we knew we weren't beating a good football team. It was all about seeing the skill and poise of Carson. It was kind of a moment of exhilaration. And we thought, this is just the very, very beginning.

"As the season went on, I was disappointed in our play at wide receiver. We could have also protected Carson better up front.[3] Our confidence in Carson is long term. We must surround him really well and build around him in the next couple of seasons and deploy our assets, draft well, definitely do things with the guy at quarterback in mind. It's a formidable task. It doesn't just happen."

* * *

After Wentz's rookie season, one of Philadelphia's first and most impressive free agent signings was the tall and talented Pro Bowl receiver Alshon Jeffrey. They made another bold free agent move with Wentz in mind when they signed bruising veteran and highly productive running back LeGarrette Blount. They love the potential balance of Blount pounding it to match Wentz slinging it. Philadelphia followed that with the signing of veteran receiver Torrey Smith. And the Eagles sought more help for Wentz in the 2017 draft with fourth round picks for receiver Mack Hollins and running back Donnel Pumphrey, as well as their fifth-round pick, receiver Shelton Gibson.

Lurie insists that the coaching around Wentz remains consistent. For now, with a season of "Start Him" complete, Lurie

---

3. Of the 85 quarterbacks who started 10+ games as a rookie, Wentz ranked 15th (tie) with 33 sacks. The reigning champ is David Carr, who was sacked 76 times with the Houston Texans in 2002, which is 20 more than the second closest.

reflects and is glad his team went from draft spots 13 to 8 to 2 to find the Eagles' potential franchise quarterback. Wentz wears No. 11. But the Eagles want him to become the No. 1 face of the franchise for many years . . .

"Again, we don't know that Carson is a franchise quarterback," Lurie said. "No one knows that right now. We believe he is. And a big part of the future defining us is we want players surrounding Carson that want to share in his incredible love for the game, his toughness, and his mental strength. Players we hope to pair with him for a long, long time. Anyone can say that, but we are going to be disciplined about that. This is a characteristic we want to identify our football team. We want that competition, that aggressive mentality spread throughout our locker room."

Lurie insists that what Wentz showed him, as well as all of the Eagles and Philadelphia fans in his rookie season, is that he craves being exceptional. He loves being committed. That he has a perfectionist spirit.

"I look forward to seeing how that plays out for him and for us year after year," Lurie said. "Carson's persona is special, it's a certain humility, a high intelligence. It's beyond the physical talent and the way he connects with his teammates. I don't see that fluctuating as we go forward. He knows the role of leadership at quarterback. Time will tell if it was worth it, but as we sit here today, our future looks bright."

Start Him. The Eagles did. All 16 games for Wentz as a starting, rookie franchise quarterback.

Wentz reflects and rejoices that it went this way. That he has deftly moved from country to urban, Eagles style.

"This is exciting," Wentz said. "This is my new home. I think we're building a team that fights to the end. That's something I want to be a part of. That's where I fit right in."

* * *

Lurie and the Eagles accepted that their quarterback situation for the long term did not include a franchise quarterback answer. They scoured the college landscape and identified Wentz as their answer. They spent draft capital to get him and were fortunate the Rams preferred Jared Goff.

They believed what they saw in Wentz from his earliest Eagles practices and classroom habits. They were impressed with his mental football capacities. They trusted what they saw and dealt Bradford. They then tossed Wentz in.

They were patient with Wentz. In the 2017 season, they will look for more growth. And success.

This is a formula many NFL executives prefer for grooming rookie quarterbacks.

In the 2017 draft, the Giants selected quarterback Davis Webb in the third round and hope he can sit behind Eli Manning and learn. But Giants general manager Jerry Reese said, just like for the Eagles, every NFL season provides surprises.

"For the Eagles and Wentz, they did it their way, and the beauty of the National Football League is that every team is going to do it their way, whatever they think is the best way," Reese said. "Sometimes there are things in this league that you don't have, there are luxuries you cannot afford, and sometimes you have to play your rookie quarterback and just protect him the best way you can. It's all about your situation."

For Wentz and the Eagles, thus far, it's a good one.

* * *

Carson Wentz completed the most passes by a rookie quarterback in NFL history (379) and tossed the second-most passes by a rookie in NFL history (607).[4]

A crucial point—Wentz started all 16 games and was strong enough physically and stout enough mentally to endure.

That is the foundation that the Eagles can feel giddy about as Wentz moves forward. Everything he did in his first NFL season was, of course, a first-time NFL experience. Now he has a concrete base on which to build. That bodes well for a player who takes mental notes on everything. He pays attention to each miniscule detail.

This is the type of mental makeup a quarterback must possess if an NFL team starts him as a rookie. Sure, it helps if talent surrounds him, but that is not the decisive factor. This matters most: The body can be perfect, the arm a cannon, but if the mind is not right, the rookie quarterback will crack. He will fail.

It is fascinating that the Eagles evaluated Jared Goff and Carson Wentz and exited categorically certain that Wentz was the better quarterback. It is great fortune that despite only being able to move into the No. 2 spot in the 2016 draft that the Eagles still grabbed the quarterback they coveted.

"Some things are meant to be," Wentz explains.

And so is this—though Eagles owner Jeffrey Lurie says no one knows if Wentz is a franchise quarterback and that it takes time to prove it, several quarterback experts expect Wentz to stick. And the reasoning is not just because of his arm, but also from what they have discerned is in his heart and head.

---

4. Andrew Luck attempted 627 passes in 2012.

Chapter 2

SIT HIM?

———————

While Carson Wentz started to open the 2016 season, Jared Goff sat.

The Rams began the season sticking to their plan that Goff would initially watch, learn, and absorb. They did not waver early on despite the enticing lure of showcasing their new, prized franchise quarterback for the team's first home game in their historic return to Los Angeles.

The game and the event were still specactacles for many reasons—including Goff.

It was an 88-degree, crispy, bright afternoon when pro football returned to the Los Angeles Coliseum. After twenty-two years, the Rams were finally home. They had scrammed from St. Louis for a prodigal-son-like linkage to this striking city of glitz and grime and everything in-between. This day—September 18, 2016—was throwback, yet modern.

The Rams wore their old-school blue and yellow uniforms. Patches of the 91,046 fans strolling into the Coliseum plastered those colors onto their faces, especially the young, seeking a "new" friend. For the older generation, the Rams had been their team from 1946 to 1994, close, just like family. It was time for the Rams, facing the Seattle Seahawks, to prove these revelers' aching wait was instantly worth it.

They did. They won the game, 9–3. Rams fans hugged. They cried. The big bowl of a stadium became a group therapy session. It was the same for the Rams' owner, Stan Kroenke, their then head coach, Jeff Fisher, and general manager Les Snead. This trio celebrated just outside a Coliseum tunnel with broad smiles and back slaps.

But inside the locker room, Jared Goff—their rookie quarterback, the 2016 NFL Draft's No. 1 overall pick, a then twenty-one-year-old who the Rams had spent lavish cache in present and future draft picks to move up and acquire—dressed quietly at his locker. He did not play. In fact, during the game, he spent most of it dressed in uniform far away from the coaching action on the sideline, not even inside several of the coach-quarterback discussions that occurred during timeouts. He looked distant.

"Well, not at all during the game," Goff said that momentous afternoon, explaining his approach during the game. The Rams had evened their record at 1–1, with veteran Case Keenum as their starting quarterback.

"I can see things better, hear better, learn more when I watch and absorb it all from a distance," Goff said. "I was checking in on the headset, asking questions, staying involved that way. I was learning."

But on the other side of the country, in Philadelphia, Wentz, the pick directly after Goff, was starting. In Dallas, Cowboys rookie quarterback Dak Prescott, taken 134 picks after Goff, was also starting. Rookie quarterbacks across the league were being instantly inserted and were making noise.

The message repeatedly emanating from Fisher, from the Rams, was that Goff was not ready. He was not mentally or physically prepared to start in the NFL. And that led to speculation that Goff was dumb. That the Rams coaching staff was dumber. That the Rams had picked the wrong guy.

Goff was not happy about any inference from the Rams' coaching decision to sit him connecting to his intelligence or talent.

"Some people are going to say what they feel they have to say," he snapped back after that Seattle game.

He integrated a stone-cold glare with those words.

* * *

It crumbled for the Rams in 2016. They won their next two games to reach a 3–1 record, but dropped 10 of their last 11 games for a 4–12 finish. Fisher, who made it clear during taping of the HBO series *Hard Knocks* before the season that he would not stand for another Rams season of "7–9 bullshit," made it through 13 games: he was fired on December 12, after a 42–14 shelling by the Atlanta Falcons at the Coliseum in front of many of those same devoted Rams fans who had arrived full of verve for the team's debut three months prior.

Before his firing, Fisher made Goff the starter in Week 11, on November 20. The Rams were 4–5 and were playing at home against the Miami Dolphins. So, Goff sat for nine games and then started the final seven games of the season.

Unfortunately for Fisher and the Rams, things didn't flow as they had hoped. Goff had a completion percentage of 54.6 percent, threw more interceptions (7) than touchdowns (5), and the Rams lost all seven of his starts. It was a similar start to that of

New York Giants quarterback Eli Manning. He was the draft's No. 1 overall pick in 2004.[1] He sat and watched as Kurt Warner started the season 5–4. In Week 11, Manning became the starter and finished 1–6. Manning, of course, later became a two-time Super Bowl champion and MVP.

Rookie Comparison:
Eli Manning (2004) vs. Jared Goff (2016)

	Manning	Goff
Starts	7	7
Record	1–6	0–7
Comp	92	112
Att	188	205
Comp%	48.94	54.63
Yds	977	1089
TD	6	5
INT	9	7
QB Rating	55.2	63.6
Sack	12	26

Can Goff craft such a road?

His rookie season proved opposite of the popular pre-draft narrative for him and Wentz. Goff was from Cal (the big school), played in big games, and was predicted to be more NFL ready. Wentz was from North Dakota State (the tiny school), had played against smaller competition on a smaller stage, and needed grooming.

---

1. The Chargers drafted Eli Manning No. 1 overall, but swapped him for Phillip Rivers, who the Giants took with their No. 3 pick.

So some people said. So some people thought.

Sitting under any circumstance did not sit well with Goff. But the Rams decided they knew what was best for him and for their franchise. They wanted him to be disappointed he was not starting. They wanted him to rise and take the job, if he could.

The Rams insisted they were working their plan.

"You run the spread offense in college and you are going to have to be re-wired to run an NFL offense," Snead said. "By the time Jared got to high school, like a lot of pro quarterbacks, he quit thinking as much. The jump from high school to college can have its complexities, but it's still usually adding to what he knows. Just like riding a bike. You can get good enough at it to pop wheelies. But you get to the NFL and it's like putting training wheels on. You're going to have some growing pains before you can pop wheelies and do new tricks up here.

"I'm sure sitting for Jared was tough. I'm sure it did not taste well. It's good to have a dialogue. I always tried to be clear and concise with Jared. You need to teach a young man to fish, not feed him for a day. You're going to have to deal with adversity and seeing how they do that is part of the process, too. There is not always going to be a hug on every corner. You have to get over it, and that's what quarterbacks do—it's what they do when they throw a pick. That's the fuel you use to say 'I'm not there yet, but I'm going to figure out how to get there.'"

Did Kroenke finally force Fisher to play Goff?

"Stan is not that type of owner," Snead said. "Anytime you are dealing with a franchise quarterback the organization is involved and Stan is involved, but the head coach has a lot of responsibility to win football games and he is going to make the decisions to do that."

Snead addressed the rumored friction between him and Fisher, and how that might have impacted Goff's rookie season.

"There is a lot of stuff said on the outside Monday through Saturday of an NFL season, a lot of chatter. Then comes Sunday. Then you move on to the next game. Jeff and I discussed Jared's progress on a weekly basis. Our relationship was definitely not toxic. It did not take us where we wanted to go. You always have to look in the mirror for that. I always examine what I did yesterday that I could always do better today. Once the ship sets sail, once it leaves the dock, you're just trying to get from Point A to Point B. We definitely had some rocky seas on the trip. We were not your typical team picking No. 1 when we took Jared. We had a plan."

* * *

The Rams' plan started with the 2015 draft.

They had selected quarterback Sam Bradford with the No. 1 overall pick in 2010, but his recurring injuries induced the Rams to move on after the 2014 season.[2] The Rams tried Shaun Hill and Austin Davis and Sean Mannion. Nick Foles. Case Keenum. Of those, Keenum became the answer to building a bridge to a franchise quarterback. In 2015, the Rams were ready—but the market demand said otherwise. The Tampa Bay Buccaneers (Jameis Winston) and the Tennessee Titans (Marcus Mariota) owned the top two picks. Both needed quarterbacks. Both swiped them.

In the 2016 draft, where Goff and Wentz lurked, the Rams were ready to pounce. The Titans owned the No. 1 pick, and the

---

2. Bradford missed 15 games in four seasons with the Rams, going 18–30–1 during that time.

Rams figured since Tennessee had just drafted Mariota they would be willing to deal that pick. They were. Snead and Titans general manager Jon Robinson discussed parameters at the 2016 NFL Combine in Indianapolis. By mid-April, the trade was announced: The Rams had moved from drafting at No. 15 of the first round to the No. 1 position. They gave the Rams six picks for the deal, including their first-round pick in 2016 and first- and third-round selections in 2017.[3]

The Rams did not wait until the trade was announced to internally begin discussing the choice between Goff and Wentz.

"We left the combine and the next weekend, on back-to-back trips, we worked out Wentz in North Dakota and Jared at Cal," Snead said. "It was important to have two guys up there at quarterback that you like. That's a big part of making such a huge deal. You never know what can happen before the draft. Injury? Life just getting in the way? This isn't fantasy football. It's real life, dealing with real human beings."

The Rams could see that Wentz was well-coached and well-versed in some NFL language, but they liked the way Goff had performed at Cal in his passing game inside the 20 and inside the red zone. The Rams believed that is where the college passing game most resembles the NFL game: An area where the field is shorter and the reads are quicker and the throws must be made into tighter windows. They had seen Goff live in games, on video, and now in this workout were looking for that kind of sizzle.

---

3. On April 14, 2016, the Rams traded their first-round pick (2016), two second-round picks (2016), a third-round pick (2016), and their first- and third-round picks of 2017 to the Tennessee Titans for their 2016 first-overall pick, as well as a fourth- and sixth-round pick (2016 as well).

There was something else about their Goff visit at the Claremont Hotel in Berkley, California, which enticed them. Something more than the countless hours of video scrutiny and Rams scouts' colorful reports.

"We get to Berkley, and it is raining all day," Snead said. "Berkley sits on a hill and the water is just gushing down all day. The workout is the next morning, 9 a.m. We sit down with Jared in the hotel lobby. We are thinking we should push it back, the session, due to the weather. And Jared is very serious. He said: 'It was scheduled for 9 a.m.; I'll be there—and I hope it's raining.' You felt it. It was one thing to hear it, it was another to feel it. The next morning, it's raining. Sure enough, he has an excellent workout."

Goff would be the guy—but they would sit him to start the season, they concluded. No need to rush him, they decided. Keenum had finished the 2015 season by winning three of the team's final four games. This was perfect, they thought. Keenum starts the 2016 season. He is the bridge. Goff watches, learns, re-wires. After all, the Rams insisted they were not a "7–9 bullshit" team desperately grabbing a franchise quarterback to be instantly employed. They were a middling 7–9 team with a sticky defense, a Rookie of the Year running back in Todd Gurley, and capable special teams. There was time. Goff was the franchise quarterback and all would enjoy the bonus of patience.

The ship, however, sank. Goff was yanked aboard. He struggled—alarmingly at times. Fisher was fired. And soon after, Sean McVay, the NFL's youngest head coach (31), was hired to talk Goff's language and, more importantly, fix his game and the Rams offense.

* * *

Instant analysis after the 2016 season often concludes that Wentz is a better quarterback and prospect than Goff, and that the Rams made a mistake. No one knows that after 16 Wentz starts and seven Goff starts, but the rumblings persist.

This is the chatter in Philadelphia, where the Eagles are certain they have the better quarterback. This is the chatter in Los Angeles, where the Rams are not buying that—yet. This is a topic fueled nationally by the media and will be a focus of discussion for the 2017 season and beyond.

"Carson Wentz was in a better situation than Goff," Jon Gruden said. "The Rams offensive line was not very good.[4] They had limited receivers. That script is not yet written. I know they said Brett Favre was a bust in Atlanta in the run and shoot offense. The head coach even made fun of him. And one year later he helped turn around a franchise in Green Bay. I was there. Some teams look at quarterbacks differently. I always thought it was a good idea to do everything you could to give them a chance to be successful so you both won't be out on the street."

New Rams head coach Sean McVay agrees. His work with quarterback Kirk Cousins in Washington pushed him on the fast track to Goff. McVay promises to tailor his offense to Goff. To push Goff to his highest potential. To duplicate what the Tennessee Titans did with Marcus Mariota's development from a college spread offense to the NFL's multiple and varied offenses.

Doubts are prevalent in NFL circles about Goff's zenith.

"I just don't see a No. 1, No. 1 quarterback there," Dick Vermeil said. "I know some other teams and quarterback people

---

4. Per the rankings from profootballfocus.com, the Rams offensive line was ranked 31st in 2015, and 28th in 2016.

in the NFL who feel the same way. Now, I'm hoping for the best for the Rams. I'm hoping for the best for Jared Goff. But if you have to go on the practice field every day like they did last year to see if he can play, chances are he can't play. If it took you nine games to determine he was ready, then . . . I just think great quarterbacks have something you can't coach. It's an innate, gifted ability. There's something different. Whatever offense the Rams were running last year, even if it was the single wing, if you can throw the ball, you can throw the ball."

Vermeil watched Goff's first NFL preseason game on TV. Actually, it was Dak Prescott's, too. It was the Cowboys at the Rams on August 13 at the LA Coliseum.

"Dak stepped in there and you could see it," Vermeil said. "He threw like nine completed passes on his first few pass attempts. I turned to my wife, Carol, and said 'I don't know who this is but the kid can play!'"[5]

For other college and NFL pro quarterback gurus, there are major concerns about Goff, originating from the spread offensive system of Washington State head coach Mike Leach, the one Goff ran at Cal. It scares people that Goff has that background. One NFL head coach said: "It [the offense] has the depth of an index card." They point to quarterbacks from this system who struggled beyond college, including Tim Couch, Josh Heupel, Kliff Kingsbury, B. J. Symons, and Graham Harrell.

"It blew my mind when they [the Rams] took a guy No. 1 in the draft from a system that is not proven in the NFL," another

---

5. Prescott completed 10 of 12 passes for 139 yards and two touchdowns, with both incompletions coming on drops by Geoff Swain, in his first career preseason game.

NFL head coach said. "The first guy successful out of that system in our league will be the first."

Leach, of course, has criticized the NFL for its offensive coaching, tutoring, and grooming of quarterbacks—or lack thereof. Leach, to put it mildly, does not think the NFL is very good at it.

In a 710 ESPN Seattle radio interview in July 2016, Leach spoke openly about the league's griping, for example, about teaching his quarterbacks to take a snap from directly under the center rather than a few feet back in the shotgun formation in the spread offense:

> Like there is something magical about somebody to do that because whichever caveman invented football, they were taking snaps under center. And I'm not talking about just one scout or one person has asked me this. But somehow the insecurity that exists with some of these people and their ability to teach a quarterback to take a quarterback snap from under center I think is disturbing commentary. Every youth league coach that I've ever met has mustered the ability to teach sixth graders to take snaps under center. So, if you're a scout and if your guys at your whatever NFL team are a fraction of the coaches that you hope they're going to be, I should think that they're able to teach somebody to take a snap from under center. I mean, obviously, the guy already knows how. A chimpanzee can take the snap from under center.

The NFL's varied views on this subject are as diverse and stimulating as they are on the overall handling of rookie quarterbacks. Green Bay Packers and Super Bowl XLV winning head coach Mike McCarthy in some ways sides with Leach.

McCarthy insists that his peers should not view the spread offense as a hindrance.

"The spread offense, the run-and-shoot, whatever it is, that doesn't bother me from a quarterback's perspective," McCarthy said. "The great thing it's done for the college game is it's balanced the competition between the bigger schools and the smaller schools. I think if you start to think about quarterbacks solely from the offense they ran in college, you are starting to box yourself in. I tend to think that those types of systems enhance a good player. If anything, it shows me the variety of what he can do and gives me more ideas of what I can do with him."

The Rams viewed it all as part of the NFL learning curve for Goff. That is why, they said, they would have to "re-wire his central nervous system." Re-wiring and changing habits produces uncomfortable moments, they said. It is like a baseball hitter changing his swing.

So, sit him, the Rams insisted.

"I made a lot of effort in the locker room talking with him, encouraging him, keeping his spirits up," Rams running back Todd Gurley said. "You could tell he was hurt by not getting to play early. Something like that can work on your mind—especially when people are already calling you a bust. That's pretty unfair and pretty cruel. But it's sort of the NFL universe. And when other young quarterbacks hit it hard right out of the gate, it opens doors for others, but it makes it hard to catch up, to match it."

Goff certainly received the scrutiny that comes with being the No. 1 overall pick. But from media and fans, it grew in unusual intensity. Some Rams fans gave up on him before his first NFL pass. Reporters charted and dissected his every practice pass.

No one knows what Jared Goff is, as he has made only seven NFL starts. But like all rookie quarterbacks, he has plenty to prove. He clearly needs more stability around him now to prove it.

"Jared is a young kid with a lot on his back," Snead said. "He has always had that in high school, as a starter for Cal, and now coming to LA. He has the blonde hair, the California cool that can be misconstrued as laid back until you get to know him as we do. He has a genuine poise about life. Inside he is a warrior, a competitor, quiet and brewing. He's thrown some balls around here where we know it's traveling a little faster, a little farther. Some big-league, big-boy passes. Now we just have to watch him grow.

"You have to have that mental toughness where the last rep or the last pass, you just move on. The last season, the last criticism. If you don't have that, you will melt away. Each quarterback is different in his personality, but I describe Jared as someone I have no problem getting into the bunker with, no problem turning my back and knowing he has my backside."

* * *

Jeff Fisher took the Rams job in 2012 because he saw a franchise quarterback already in the fold.

"I loved Sam Bradford," Fisher said. "It's why I took the job, and because of the relationship with [owner] Stan [Kroenke]. It felt like the right place."

Fisher had spent most of his NFL head coaching career with the Tennessee Titans and quarterback Steve McNair. Together they reached Super Bowl XXXIV, a 23–16 loss to the then St. Louis Rams in 2000.

Twelve years later, Fisher's coaching career took this tantalizing twist to the Rams.

"We took over a 2-win team," Fisher said. "We were building."

Bradford and Fisher were 7–8–1 that first season. Then, the following year, Bradford tore his left ACL after 7 starts and missed the remainder of the season. The next year, in 2014, he tore it again during the preseason and missed the entire regular season.

Fisher said that is the road which led to Jared Goff.

"We were on the quarterback trail in 2015. It was a two-year process. We went through some quarterbacks during that time who I have a great deal of respect for; they were not Sam Bradford. In the 2015 draft, we liked Mariota and Winston. They were not going to be available in that draft (because Tampa Bay and Tennessee, who held that draft's top picks, were locked in on drafting them). I remember walking off the field in the final game of the 2015 season, an overtime loss at San Francisco. It was tough. But I also remember thinking, *Imagine, if we had won this game, we probably wouldn't be in position to move up and get a quarterback next year.* It was a very strange feeling.

"I remember the visit with Jared at Cal, his workout. It was pouring rain. I personally had balls inside my jacket, trying to keep them dry, and would hand them to the center so he could try to snap Jared a dry ball. Jared didn't care if the ball was wet or not. He just threw. Jared probably preferred it was a wet ball instead of a dry ball.

"It was a collective decision to draft Jared. We felt Jared's arm strength was just a notch above Carson's. That's why we took him. The decision to sit Jared was mine. The decision to play him when we did was mine. Both."

Fisher's experience with McNair was not the exact same model for Goff, Fisher said, nor did he attempt to perfectly duplicate it. McNair sat for his first two years as a Titan, playing sparingly, before becoming a starter in his third season.

And though it was not the same model, the McNair influence was prevalent.

"It was not the model, but it was patience," Fisher said. "This is the unique thing about the quarterback situation—the modern-day NFL quarterback, I'd say in the last fifteen years, it's not necessarily Sundays, in my opinion. It is the week, the practice week. The requests of your quarterback, the preparation, the week after week . . . if your quarterback has a bad day of practice, the rest of the team goes, 'Ugh!' They know what's going on. After the Super Bowl in 2000, Steve was going to quit. He just didn't think he could do it all any more: the grind, the pain. I made the mistake of not making those practices more fun, less stressful for him. It is not an easy job for a quarterback. It's a hard job. You got to make those practices go from week to week, adjust. And I did. And two years later he was the league co-MVP with Peyton Manning.

"Imagine that on a rookie? The pressure is immense. It is a challenge during the week to keep him whole and healthy. We were not going to put that on Jared. We were not going to cripple the player. That was our philosophy. We wanted him to experience it by watching and not have that pressure to play. And Case had won some games. He was a terrific guy, a terrific leader, a great locker room guy. It was a good situation for Jared. He was going to learn very quality NFL lessons from Case."

So, sit him, the Rams insisted.

But the Rams' move from St. Louis to Los Angeles created confusion and displacement for the entire organization—with a January announcement and a March move. The infrastructure of the move was taxing from the housing situations for all to the unstable practice and training sites to the rambunctious and distracting filming of their *Hard Knocks* (HBO) and *All or Nothing* (Amazon/NFL Films) series. They also lost valuable players, including cornerback Janoris Jenkins, to free agency.[6]

As the season spun, the Rams did not win enough games with Keenum. The Rams did not score enough points with Keenum. Gurley called it a "high school" offense. The cry for Goff increased inside and outside of the Rams building.

"Jared's and Carson's situations were altogether different," Fisher said. "We had made the decision that we had time to bring Jared along. Minnesota lost a quarterback, made a trade, and Carson got in there for Philadelphia; they were not initially planning on starting him, either. And then Carson starts 2–0 and is on fire and our guy is on the bench, a backup and inactive for the first game. He dealt with it. He is a talented, talented player. But it made it harder for him.

"Stan is not the type of owner to tell you to play a player. I personally told Stan while we were warming up for the Jets game [in Week 10] in New York that Jared was going to start the next week against Miami at home. We beat the Jets. We were coming off a win in New York. I had a meeting with the quarterbacks when we returned. Jared had gone from being inactive the first week to running the scout team to gradually getting more and more reps and, as we pushed along, Week 11 became the time.

---

6. In March 2016, Janoris Jenkins signed a five-year, $62.5 million contract with the New York Giants, and made his first Pro Bowl appearance.

"Jared was not drafted because he was from California. He was not drafted as a marketing tool. We didn't give so much to trade up to get him to look cool. I told Stan, forget we are moving to Los Angeles, we would be doing this if we were still in St. Louis. It was never an LA thing. It was the best thing for the Rams."

Jon Gruden and others in and around the NFL have heard the narrative that Fisher waited that long—and would have waited longer—to try and buy more time to coach the struggling Rams. To hold onto the Goff card as long as possible, as a reason for a Fisher return for the 2017 season.

Gruden calls that "barbershop talk." He added: "These coaches want to win. They will do anything to get a first down, let alone win a game. I don't believe that for a second about Jeff Fisher."

Fisher bluntly responded to that stinging narrative: "I have never been a coach who looked over my shoulder. Every year you have to win. I never felt starting this quarterback or sitting this quarterback saves my job. I looked at the mental, emotional, and physical toll on Jared and was not going to be in a hurry. We were building for the future. There was no friction in the building in relation to the quarterback; we were on the same page. It was not a factor as far as Jared was concerned. Young quarterbacks need help. They play against really good defenses. They need a running game. The kid [Dak Prescott] at Dallas can play, but he had that. I take responsibility for us not having that. But there were certainly a lot of factors across the board involved in that, too.

"If I had it to do over, I wouldn't do it differently. There are some things that were unavoidable. There are some things that you don't like, too, for your rookie quarterback. He's in a blimp (during the filming of *Hard Knocks* where Goff is asked about the direction of the sunrise and the sunset, and Goff is confused). They ask him the East-West thing and where the sun comes up.

It's his day off. Dak Prescott did not do that. It's good copy. It's great video. It's a fun story. But a young quarterback just needs to focus on football. Just relax. He's tough. He got even tougher. He got hit early in the preseason games, I mean from his ribcage to the bottom of his ass cheek was black and blue! He did not miss a minute, not a day of practice after that. It's highly unlikely anyone saw that contusion or even knew. People don't see that about him. People don't know that about him."

Fisher said Goff's spread offensive background was not an issue for him. He loves Goff's vision, his release, his height [6-foot-4]. He can see, Fisher said. He can throw. He is willing to prepare. He likes his footwork, his pocket presence, his arm. He *really* loves his arm.

"I didn't pay much attention to the last four weeks of the season," Fisher said. "It's their issue, not mine. Unfortunately, I was let go and I won't be a part of his future. But I think Jared is going to be successful depending on what the rest of the team does. Wade Phillips as the defensive coordinator there will do a great job because he's been good wherever he's been. Jared has to have a running game. He needs a play-action pass game off that running game. I'm hoping for the best for Jared. We made a commitment to him. I honestly don't think it will be his fault if he doesn't make it. If he doesn't get the other pieces around him and struggles, that is not his fault."

* * *

On January 12, 2017, Sean McVay was hired as the Rams new head coach. McVay then was age thirty. That made him eight years older than Jared Goff and twenty-nine years younger than Fisher. McVay chose Wade Phillips as his defensive coordinator. Phillips is seventy years old. Even Phillips jumped in on the age thing with this cracking tweet soon after his hire: "Rams have the only staff with DC on Medicare and HC in Daycare."

McVay became the youngest head coach in modern NFL history. Two weeks after his hire, he turned thirty-one.

His age as part of his selection was not an accident. Owner Stan Kroenke and the Rams decided to invest in their colossal investment, in Goff, by connecting him with a fresh offensive mind and a head coach closer to Goff's generation.

"Sure, we talked about a lot of things during the interview process, but the real points were that I have an offensive philosophy that we operated in Washington where everything starts with the quarterback," McVay said. "My experience with coach [Jay] Gruden and coach [Bill] Walsh, and with my grandfather [John] McVay, a former San Francisco 49ers general manager who helped build five Super Bowl championship teams] showed me that quarterback is the most difficult job in sports. And the most important one.

"You hear defensive coaches say they want to make offenses earn every blade of grass. Well, we want to make defenses defend every blade of grass. We want to use the width and depth of the field. Use the run game. Mix personnel groups. Actually, it boils down to the staple of every great coach: See what any player does best and fit the skill to the offense. You have to figure that out before you go into a season."

McVay said he sees why Goff was a No. 1 overall draft pick. He also does not see Goff's spread offensive background as a roadblock.

"When you really look at it, the spread system is on the rise in college. You see more coming into the NFL as of late. The spread sample size is growing. Marcus Mariota came from it and he's playing at a high level. It's not that those guys can't do it. There is still a reluctance in the NFL about it even though high school and college football are using it. But those are the guys coming out. You have to adjust.

"We are going to figure out what Jared is most comfortable with and what he does best. He's going to be taught every day. I see some physical attributes and traits that are there. The real challenge is to find out how to materialize them. I've seen him throw from different platforms. I've seen him change delivery at the top when needed."

He's seen him take some brutal shots, too. Some nasty in-game hits.

"I see an extremely tough guy. Some of his games from last year, he took some serious shots. I love the way he responded. Especially in his games against Atlanta and New Orleans. This is a trait essential to quarterbacking. It's not necessarily taught. You are fearless in that pocket or you are not."

McVay said everyone should realize that since he was not around for Goff's rookie season, he does not know the intricate particulars of why Goff sat, why he was inserted in Week 11, or if that plan was best. He said the fact that rookies Carson Wentz in Philadelphia and Dak Prescott in Dallas started was more a credit to those players and to those coaching staffs than an indictment on Goff and the Rams, because the "situations and the blueprints were totally different."

McVay's focus is on building a Goff identity, a Rams identity. He paid close attention to what Atlanta Falcons coach Dan

Quinn created in 2016 in their Super Bowl–appearing season. McVay said the tape showed him that Quinn built a team that cared about playing for each other and played collectively as complementary pieces. It became their identity, he said, and it served them well.

It is a noteworthy model, he said.

Some Washington Redskins sources said that Goff had better look out. That McVay will not walk into the place trying to prove himself to Goff. That Goff will be coached hard and will have to prove himself to McVay. And if not, McVay will not hesitate on insisting that the Rams move on.

McVay did not deny that, but he did insist that his approach will not be that hammering, that all-or-else.

"The standard here is to be detailed and precise right away," McVay said. "I expect to be held accountable on the things we have agreed upon and I expect the same as well. We will do it all in a positive way. Jared did not gain the experience some other rookie quarterbacks did last year, but he did play and he'll take the good and the bad and learn from it, grow from it. We will focus on him being receptive on retention, on his comprehension. The quarterback needs help. But you go as the quarterback goes."

* * *

The views on Jared Goff are assorted. He can play. He can't play. He should have started right away. He was well served by sitting initially. "He is slow as a snail," said one NFL head coach. "He is more than nimble enough," said another.

The Rams went all in, maneuvered for the 2016 draft's top pick and took Goff. They have changed head coaches and direction since then. But like Wentz in Philly, a major goal is to improve the cast around Goff in LA. In free agency, the Rams swiped receiver Robert Woods and Pro Bowl tackle Andrew Whitworth. They used their first three picks in the 2017 draft with Goff in mind by selecting tight end Gerald Everett and receivers Cooper Kupp and Josh Reynolds. They followed that by later drafting fullback Sam Rogers.

The Rams are hoping a fresh approach brings the best from Goff. This young quarterback is driven to turn it around, catch up, and surpass Wentz. The two are and will be forever linked. They even share the same agents.

Wentz started.

Goff sat.

Wentz has the same head coach. Goff has a new one. Those relationships will help define their careers.

* * *

Behind the scenes, there was plenty of havoc bubbling among the Rams ownership, management, and coaches well before the Rams even drafted Jared Goff. The strain of the move from St. Louis to Los Angeles and the differing views on veteran personnel decisions caused both confusion and conflict.

But the Rams navigated through that and together made the choice that Goff was their franchise quarterback. They firmly decided he was the answer for their future.

It appears they may have been shocked, once he was in the fold, at just how much grooming was required.

"I'm told," said one NFL head coach, "that the Rams were afraid of him completely embarrassing himself and them even in the preseason games because he was so unready. I don't think they tried to shelter him early in their season—I think they tried to literally hide him."

We don't know that, but we do know that the Rams did not think Goff was ready to start, did not plan for him to start, and instead chose the option of a veteran quarterback who would build a bridge to Goff. That bridge was Case Keenum.

The Rams offense, however, was so ineffective as the season unfolded that the Rams became stuck with a veteran quarterback who was not producing and a rookie quarterback who was not ready. An NFL team must sit a rookie quarterback who is not ready. But some ask, how do you know if they are ready if you don't play them? Well, the practices don't lie. The practice tape doesn't lie. And his teammates aren't dumb.

Given how it all disintegrated for the Rams in 2016, it is hard to believe that they would do it again in the same manner. It is hard to fathom that they wouldn't have started Goff, shaved the playbook, and hoped for a different outcome.

If you are going to start a rookie quarterback, a proper trek is to reduce the playbook, concentrate on a handful of plays he executes best, and build the offense slowly. Rely on the running game and defense and special teams and, literally, groom the rookie quarterback in the actual games. That is unless he soars in mental NFL aptitude and talent. Most rookies don't. So, pare it and play him and groom him, or, simply, take all of the lumps that can come with sitting him.

Sometimes NFL coaches and franchises need to exhibit as much backbone as they expect from these potential franchise quarterbacks.

Hall of Fame defensive end/linebacker Charles Haley, the first NFL five-time Super Bowl champion (who won two with the

49ers and three with the Cowboys), examined his championship success in Dallas.

"Look, we had good defense and special teams and that's important in a championship but, hey, I won Super Bowls with Joe Montana and Troy Aikman as quarterbacks," Haley said. "That's Hall of Fame quarterbacking. You're just not going to get to that game and win that game without your quarterback doing something great. But here's the thing I've never understood about what the league does with rookie quarterbacks: They bring them in, load them down with these big, huge playbooks and have them bogged down and thinking so much instead of just playing the game.

"In Dallas, Troy had 10 or 12 plays. The offense had 10 or 12 plays. Those were the focus. Those were the plays they practiced and perfected. They had the talent, but they also got so good at those plays that nobody could stop them. And the NFL should do more of that with rookie quarterbacks. Cut the shit and find out what the guy does best and just give him a handful of plays to run. And perfect them. I really believe a lot of rookie quarterbacks would thrive with that type of approach and in that type of system. Stop complicating the game so much. Keep it simple, stupid."

Goff could join a long list of big-name quarterbacks who sat at the start only to stand in the end. It is also possible that his struggles have only just begun. He will have the chance with a new head coach, a new offense, and more weapons around him to prove his mettle.

There is an amazing array of people across the NFL spectrum who doubt he can. Goff can craft the last word.

Chapter 3

THE HEAD COACH AND QUARTERBACK RELATIONSHIP

There are three areas which are crucial for a franchise quarterback to thrive: leadership, communication and a reliable relationship with his head coach. Faulty command in any of these areas can torpedo the quarterback and his team.

The players expect him to lead. They want him to find a way to connect—even in a small way—with every teammate in the locker room. Coaches expect him to be able to communicate what he sees on the field at all times. They expect him to be able to challenge his teammates as much as praise them.

The head coach and quarterback do not require a social, family-oriented, vacation-time relationship. But there must be mutual respect. Direct, honest communication. And some semblance of fun mixed with passion in a game they both love.

"I'm watching, the players are watching his leadership skills," Jon Gruden said. "If he can't communicate, not only verbal but non-verbal, he has no chance. And certainly, he has to be the extension, the ambassador of the head coach. If the team is the reflection of the head coach, the quarterback has to be the strongest reflection."

These areas are minefields, especially for rookie quarterbacks quickly granted the keys to the franchise. He enters with veteran players looking at him sideways, concerned their season is at stake while he painstakingly learns—he has time on his side, they do not. The fan base critiques his every pass, decision, and on- and off-field moves. The media does the same.

The head coach tries to keep him on track, balanced, sane . . . while still pushing him.

"These are all important factors," Bill Belichick said. "Each individual player is different and each person has their own way of developing and connecting to his teammates."

That "way" must provide a leadership/communication model which clicks with the players and works for the coach, regardless of their individuality. Belichick also noted that the maturity of the rookie quarterback is important in this process.

* * *

A rookie quarterback's maturity level walking through the door and how it develops during the scope of that season and his career is defining.

Hall of Fame quarterback Bart Starr exemplifies this. He joined the Green Bay Packers in 1956, and was a pillar of their dominating five-time championship teams until retiring in 1971. He also won the first two Super Bowl MVP awards.

Starr described his relationship with his coach, Vince Lombardi, as grinding and tough, especially early on. Lombardi rode Starr hard. But as their time together grew, Lombardi realized that the burden

Starr carried as the franchise quarterback was enormous. The Hall of Fame head coach said he learned to focus more on relaxing his quarterback than intensely demanding his leadership and communication. Lombardi realized he already had all of that in Starr.

In a piercing revelation, Lombardi explained it this way in *Bart Starr: When Leadership Mattered*, by David Claerbaut:

"Without a good quarterback, you just don't operate. Bart Starr stands for what the game of football stands for: courage, stamina, and coordinated efficiency. You instill desire by creating a superlative example. The noblest form of leadership is by example, and that is what Bart Starr is about."

Starr's teammates consistently offered matching prophetic and sincere analysis of him.

Hall of Fame quarterback Roger Staubach (1969–79) had a similar experience with the Dallas Cowboys and his Hall of Fame head coach, Tom Landry. Their respect for each other as men first and then as leaders of the Cowboys was a constant, dual reflection that permeated the entire Cowboys franchise and helped build their brand as "America's Team."

Competition between quarterbacks can also help build a team's success. The Joe Montana-Steve Young duel in San Francisco in 1992 under head coach George Seifert was a fiery relationship among eventual Hall of Fame quarterbacks. Montana won three Super Bowls under Hall of Fame coach Bill Walsh (1981, 1984, 1988), and one under Seifert (1989). Young won his under Seifert (1994).

"Bill was a coach who when he just walked through the locker room among the players, you could hear a pin drop," former 49ers safety Ronnie Lott said. "He had that kind of respect. I spent all of my time there with Joe as our guy. After I left for the Raiders, that competition between Joe and Steve took off. But the thing was both were great leaders and communicators. Both ran the offense the way the 49ers wanted it. That's why both of them were so successful. It was a rich time for the 49ers because the franchise quarterback was never a question. It was only which one."

Sometimes a rookie quarterback arrives in the NFL from a small place and winds up in a big spot with big dreams. Carson Wentz is one of the latest. And Doug Williams in 1978 steered that path, moving from Grambling to the Tampa Bay Buccaneers.

Williams was a four-year starter at Grambling under iconic head coach Eddie Robinson, going 36–7 (a .837 winning percentage) as the school's quarterback. He was a first-round pick, No. 17, in the 1978 NFL Draft. The Buccaneers were an expansion team two years prior and were 0–14 and 2–12 in those seasons. Williams started 10 games his rookie season, the Bucs improved to 5–11, and the season afterward he turned them into a playoff bunch. In 1988, he led the Washington Redskins to a Super Bowl XXII victory and became the first African American quarterback to win a Super Bowl.

His NFL teammates and coaches in both cities, as well as with both teams, applauded his leadership and communication. After retiring from the league, he continued to display that leadership as a college head coach and an NFL executive. He is currently a personnel executive for the Redskins.

Williams says the relationships with his head coaches and their influence—John McKay in Tampa Bay and Joe Gibbs in Washington—were powerful.

"John McKay gave me confidence. No matter what was going on, he stressed confidence. 'Don't worry about it Dougie!' he used to say. 'What happened on that play Dougie? Here's how we'll fix it.' I later found out that if he put an 'ie' at the end of your name, he really liked you. Joe Gibbs was the offensive coordinator during my first year in Tampa. I used to go home with him and eat dinner with his family and study my playbook. After dinner he would drive me back to training camp. Then we later connected in Washington to make some history.

"The role of the head coach and the quarterback has changed drastically since that time. They both sort of take the position as CEOs. But somewhere in there, you've got to let the quarterback know you believe in him. And the quarterback better let the head coach know he believes in him. This is how the coaching takes root."

This was the kind of relationship Randall Cunningham had with Buddy Ryan.

The two intersected from 1986–90, with Cunningham as the Philadelphia Eagles quarterback and Ryan the head coach. Ryan created an us-against-the-world mentality with his young quarterback, who had been drafted in the second round (No. 37 overall) by the Eagles in 1985. Ryan even built that theme in the Eagles offices with an approach that made his team almost insular from management, a "downstairs, us, and those guys upstairs, management and ownership" split, he would say. Cunningham bought in and played the position with dramatic flair.

"Buddy treated us as his children," Cunningham said. "He made you want to go all-in on the field for him. We had a strong bond and sense of team."

Jeff Fisher, a Ryan disciple, built a lasting bond with his franchise quarterback, Steve McNair. McNair came to the then Houston Oilers and soon Tennessee Titans from tiny Alcorn State in 1995 (drafted No. 3 overall). The Fisher-McNair connection lasted ten years, with several signature NFL victories and moments. Sadly, McNair was murdered in 2009.

"I think about him every day," Fisher said. "Every situation with a rookie franchise quarterback is different. Steve didn't start until his third year. He played some in year one and two, gained valuable experience, but we wanted him to get a foundation—an NFL foundation. Sure, he wanted to play his rookie year. But you know what he also said? 'I'm going to play when the coach says I can play.' That's what he said. That's the type of leader, that's the type of communication you want from your franchise quarterback. His teammates noticed it. They respected him for it. And when he got in there, they followed him to the wall."[1]

* * *

The 1999 season presented teams in the NFC Championship game that rode young quarterbacks. Shaun King was a rookie with Tampa Bay, while Kurt Warner was in his second season with St. Louis after throwing only 11 passes as a rookie. Warner was an undrafted free agent signee by Green Bay in 1994, who was later cut, stocked groceries at a supermarket, and played in the Arena Football League and NFL Europe before becoming an NFL rookie in 1998 that stuck on with the Rams at the age of twenty-seven. He is now a Hall of Famer.

Both King and Warner in the '99 season saw the starting quarterbacks ahead of them injured. For King with the Buccaneers,

---

1. McNair started only six games his first two seasons in the league, going 4–2 (2–0 his rookie season and 2–2 the following year).

it was Trent Dilfer with a broken clavicle in Week 12 at Seattle. For Warner with the Rams, it was Trent Green with a torn ACL during the preseason.

Both guided their teams to the playoffs with dynamic play, leadership, communication, and were reflections of their head coaches.

"We were in that boat, looking for a franchise quarterback, thinking that down the road we had to move on from Trent Dilfer," Tony Dungy said of his Bucs. "We drafted Shaun in the second round in 1999 from Tulane because he had the skills and his leadership and communication components were impressive. And, sure enough, Trent [Dilfer] gets hurt. Shaun jumps in there, and we go on one of those magical runs.[2] Now, Shaun in that draft in '99 was with Tim Couch, Donovan McNabb, Akili Smith, and Daunte Culpepper. I think they were 1, 2, 3, and 11, in that order, before Shaun, in the first round. Shaun was a second round pick, No. 50. That's how it goes sometimes; the guy on the back end at the start, on the field, jumps over all the guys in front of him. Sometimes it lasts, sometimes it doesn't.

"The thing we liked about Shaun, too, was he was just a winner. He rallied people. He wasn't that tall. He didn't have a cannon arm. He just made plays and won games. He got into the lineup and he was cool, unflappable. He didn't play like a rookie. He had a good defense supporting him. But the thing he exuded the most was, 'I know what I'm doing' and 'You guys can believe in me.' That ability, to get the players, to get the coaches to believe you can do the right thing at the right time is something special."

---

2. With King as the starter, the Bucs went 4–1 to end the season with an 11–5 record.

The Rams won that NFC title game, 11–6, and would go on to win Super Bowl XXIV against the Titans. When Trent Green was lost, Rams head coach Dick Vermeil emotionally explained that the Rams would go with Warner and simply do the best they could. Warner threw 41 touchdown passes and won 13 regular season games on the way to the championship.

"Kurt played as well or better in games than he did in practice," Vermeil said. "But there was always this intrinsic thing he showed about playing quarterback that eventually made us believe what we saw. After a few practices, when he took over for Trent [Green], he kept winning in those practices against our defense. And finally, I'm walking off the field and I'm thinking, *Man, either our defense stinks or this kid can play.* I think that's the thing with young quarterbacks, the thing to remember as a coach. When you see a young quarterback do things that startle you, try to give him an opportunity to do it often.

"There's just something about a franchise quarterback, even a young one. There is something about that guy. None of us can really describe it. We've never truly been able to define it. But you know it when you see it. And the players know it. They can feel it."

* * *

A handful of young franchise quarterbacks in today's game are making similar marks. They are excelling at leadership and communication with their teammates. Their head coaches connect with them. The vibe when they are in the locker room oozes acceptance.

Appreciation.

Respect and belief.

This is happening with Derek Carr in Oakland.

With Carr, who was drafted in the second round (No. 36 overall) in the 2014 draft, the 2016 Raiders won 12 games, scored an AFC-second-best 416 points, and made the playoffs.[3] Unfortunately for the Raiders, Carr was lost during their Week 15 game against the Colts when he broke his fibula, ending his season early. The Raiders lost the final game of the season against the Broncos and their first-round playoff match against the Texans. Not only did they lose, they looked lost without their young quarterback.

It was his talent, his performance, his leadership, his communication. Only age twenty-six, only in his third season, his play, voice, and impact are cemented among the Raiders, among his teammates.

He sets that Bart Starr–like example.

After a Week 13 victory over the Buffalo Bills in Oakland on December 4, Raiders star receiver Amari Cooper stood at his locker and described Carr's early-game day preparation: "I come early and I see him here, too. I see Derek sitting there with a notebook of plays and looking over everything that we are going to call during the game. He's making sure he knows what each receiver has, so, that's why I'm not surprised by his success. I wouldn't call it cramming because he is diligent throughout the week as well."

His ability to connect with his teammates is as impressive as his preparation. Raiders running back Taiwan Jones said Carr makes sure the Raiders are not a team of cliques. After a Wednesday

---

3. It was the team's first winning season since 2002, when they lost in Super Bowl XXXVII to the Buccaneers.

practice late in the 2016 season, Jones said this about Carr before leaving the Raiders facility:

"Our quarterback, you can see his values, he cares about everyone including the guys on the practice squad. He is the kind of leader that has built this team into a real team."

Carr embraces the role. The Raiders embrace him.

His impact in the locker room was evident after that victory over the Bills. He covered a lot of ground in the locker room, just milling from teammate to teammate. They discussed the game. They chatted about the future.

"We have a good group," Carr said. "We have a lot of talk that goes on. A lot of communication goes on in the huddle, which is awesome. I love to communicate. I love to talk about what's going on in the situation. When the momentum is starting to build, I try to get everyone to take a deep breath. We all take a deep breath and make sure we're signed and sound. Let's make sure we don't forget the little details with our mind being on the big play that just happened."

He is a veritable reflection of his head coach, Jack Del Rio.

"I think we've changed the mentality here and Derek is a big part of that," Del Rio said.

He is so much a part of it that the Raiders recently signed Carr to a five-year, $125 million-plus contract that makes him the first NFL player to earn $25 million or more per season.

* * *

Jameis Winston started as a rookie for the Tampa Bay Buccaneers, and has started all 32 games of his NFL career. He was the No. 1 overall pick in 2015. He expected nothing less.

In middle school, he created a quarterback notebook that included plays drawn, situations covered, formations, and routes examined. And he created this—his list of traits essential for a quarterback:

Leadership

Dedication

Desire

Student

Mental Toughness

Character

Confidence

Entering the 2017 NFL season at only twenty-three years of age, Winston is exhibiting each of those traits, according to his head coach Dirk Koetter.

"Every quarterback is different. You get drafted first, you usually are not going to a team that is good. But we've grown. We couldn't be more excited with Jameis. Our guys did so much background on Jameis. All of it is coming true."

Mike Mularkey, the Titans head coach, thinks of his quarterback in comparable ways. Marcus Mariota was drafted one slot behind Winston in 2015.

"I think the thing we've seen with Marcus is he listens, he learns, and he shares that knowledge with his teammates. He is a leader in the truest definition of the word. He communicates extremely well with his teammates. He's likeable. And his ability is coming to the surface daily."

These young quarterbacks and their coaches are chasing the pinnacle quarterback-head coach pair in the league: Tom Brady and Bill Belichick of the New England Patriots. Together, they have won five Super Bowls. Tough to duplicate. So is their working relationship.

* * *

The Patriots' dynastic string was kindled by a quarterback with big dreams and extreme focus, the kind that would match his new coach and owner.

Tom Brady strolled into the Patriots' den in 2000 from the University of Michigan, a sixth-round pick with the mindset, leadership, and communication skills of a No. 1 guy. He was never the most athletically talented, but he was always the most focused, the most determined. A young man with vision—and guts.

He told Patriots owner Bob Kraft when he first met him that Kraft had just made the smartest decision and the best pick ever, and that he would not regret it. Kraft said that there was something about the moment, the words that stuck with him. Something in Brady's eyes. In his voice. Something that made Kraft believe him. An instinct. A feeling.

Five Super Bowl championships later, all of it has been cemented.

Brady entered as the fourth of four quarterbacks on the Patriots 2000 roster. In the Patriots draft room, when the fifth round arrived, Belichick asked, "What is Brady still doing on the board?" And Belichick said that if he was still there in the sixth round, the Patriots would take him. And so they did. Belichick knew Brady had value, but even he did not know how immense, how grand that value would prove.

Brady arrived as a rookie and immediately went to work. No, actually, he worked his tail off. He was in the Patriots building early and he stayed late. He was particularly close with starter Drew Bledsoe. Everybody in the building knew Bledsoe, who had been the team's starter since 1993. Brady was just some kid from Michigan. Within a year he had moved from the fourth quarterback on the depth chart to the backup spot. And when Bledsoe was injured in Week 2 of 2001, Brady took over. He went 11–3 to finish the regular season, and led the Patriots to victory in Super Bowl XXXVI against the Rams. He took the job and kept the job.

For those first three or four seasons, Brady was a sponge at Belichick's feet. Brady was already football savvy. Now he was learning to match brainpower with Belichick. He was becoming a mirror, a reflection of his head coach.

They began to meet on Tuesdays to dissect opposing teams. To discuss their personnel. To strategize. Belichick has seen Brady grow so knowledgeable, so full of wisdom that the coach knew he better come fully prepared to those meetings, because Brady now knew it like an offensive coordinator. Like a head coach. These meetings have now evolved into more give and take than pupil-teacher.

That is one way Brady has become an effective leader for the Patriots. He has little patience for teammates who don't know the offense, who don't know their roles, who don't know the plays, who wind up in the wrong spots. He has become a player/coach on the field who directly challenges his teammates. Get prepared. Stay prepared. Execute.

Brady has the analytics, the mental acumen and book on opponents and their coaches, the data of 12 AFC Championship games and 7 Super Bowls and all before and in-between and afterward. He effectively is a coach—Belichick's reflection.

The meticulous detail of Bill Belichick, a lifetime of coaching, a memory bank of detailed football situations that he uses to craft, mold, and coach his team is just how Tom Brady plays quarterback. Yet, they are somewhat the antithesis of each other.

Brady is a man of social graces, of overt empathy, a guy you would be delighted that your daughter is marrying. Belichick can be charming, enduring, but he's a guy you might initially think your daughter is nuts for marrying. Both are great fathers. Both are great football men.

They employ a relationship of respect more than coziness and fuzziness. They complement each other's brilliance. The leadership, the communication, the reflection for Tom Brady is organic and significant.

Their results are a cunning model, the envy of the league.

The Seattle Seahawks, however, present a quarterback-head coach duo that also is striking in results and noteworthy in reflection.

* * *

Russell Wilson is twenty-eight years old. He is 5-foot-11, 215 pounds. Wilson was a 2012 third-round pick, selection No. 175. He is the Seattle Seahawks' franchise quarterback.

Wilson started all 16 games as a rookie in 2012, and threw 26 touchdown passes. He won Super Bowl XLVIII in 2014, and returned for an encore appearance the following season in a loss to Tom Brady's Patriots. His 46 victories in his first four seasons are the most any quarterback has amassed in an opening four-year span in NFL history. He is also the second-highest-rated passer in NFL history, trailing only Green Bay's Aaron Rodgers.

His leadership skills are strong. So is his communication and his reflection of Seattle head coach Pete Carroll, winner of Super Bowl XLVIII.

Wilson exudes confidence.

"John Schneider, our GM, really loved the guy," Carroll recalls of Seattle's 2012 draft process. "He loved the athleticism. As we began to scout him, he blew us away, the natural competitor he was. He has unique qualities. Great athlete. Ability to throw the ball in different body positions in and out of the pocket and on the run. I was hearing special things about his character, but early in the scouting process we hadn't nailed that down yet. People were talking about how short he was and how that would translate to the NFL game. There was this and that, but we loved the player.

"When he went to Wisconsin, they made him captain after three weeks. He built up a lot of positives. I'm not concerned when we draft a guy out of profile. You want him to fit the profile first. If not, what is it about the guy that makes you want to take closer look."

Carroll first met Wilson at the 2012 Senior Bowl.

"He had a baseball background. I loved that; just more versatility. Someone had warned me that when I met him to be prepared that things he would say he totally believed. To not take it the wrong way. It's just his confidence, his way. So, he walks into our hotel room for a visit and says he is going to be All-Pro. Win the Super Bowl. I didn't say OK, sure, but just, OK, OK, OK. He was really confident and bold with a big-picture outlook. He allowed himself to be inspired."

Carroll immediately realized they shared "an outlook of optimism." That, when the games are long and tough, they both believe those games can be won.

But that Wilson confidence which was explained to Carroll before their first meeting, the way that Carroll prepped for it, did not flow that easily for Wilson's teammates in their earliest phases with him. They initially saw Wilson as "a different kind of cat," one of his current teammates said.

There was a confidence about him, yet, he was too easily, too naturally of a self-aggrandizing nature, other teammates said. The Seahawks initially produced too much team success cloaked into Wilson, where the players were beginning to feel like they were the "Russell Wilsons" instead of the Seattle Seahawks.

Too much marketing of his brand sometimes at the expense of their own.

Too much "Russell being Russell."

"Early on I talked to him," Carroll said. "I talked to other quarterbacks I've had, to Matt Leinart and Carson Palmer and all the others. That you and I must represent this team. Be connected in our understanding and our language. That I'm counting on you. We give each other great support. We operate in concert. He has totally bought in. It's expected. We both have so many opportunities to represent the team. We sort of do as one.

"When our program first started here in Seattle, a lot of our guys were the same age. All of them were in one or two years of each other. A lot of elite players in the league. A lot happening all of the time. Going through changes. A lot of people blossoming at different times. The quarterback is going to get a lot of the focus. And Russell did. There was some stuff to work out, because the really good quarterbacks are unique. They have their own way of doing things. They are not always clicking with everybody. They have so much going on in the way they are overwhelmingly involved. Maybe one day they blow through the locker room with a hundred things on their minds. And maybe they didn't say hello to someone. So much on their minds, yet, scrutinized. Favre, Peyton, Brady, they're all like that.

"I was in the quarterback room before Russell came to his first minicamp. I told the guys not to expect this guy to be one of the fellas. He's on a destiny trip. He may surprise you. Give it some time to figure it out. I want everyone here to be themselves. Now, Russell is older. The younger guys on the team see him much differently from the guys he grew up with here. The younger guys grew up watching him on TV. He had a date with destiny in his mind. I hoped it was real. One practice and he showed command. He was just centered, extraordinary. We said yeah, we can see how it happened at Wisconsin with him."

Carroll insists that the NFL is, first and foremost, a relationship business. And that is his philosophy in Seattle. It is just who the Seahawks are, he says. He said his coaches coach with development principles in mind. He tells them all to celebrate uniqueness. He tells them everyone finds their best when they learn how to deal with each other.

"We went through his rookie preseason evaluating him and Matt Flynn. It was a structured, competitive format. The fourth preseason game, against Kansas City, I think he scored five out of the first six times we had the ball. I remember telling our coaches: 'It looks like we are going to do it. We got a rookie starter.' [General Manager] John [Schneider] wanted to ease into the situation. He thought it might be too much too soon for Russell. But we compete. He won the competition. He's the starter.'"

Carroll turns sixty-six on September 15. He is thirty-seven-plus years older than Russell, and the league's oldest head coach. He had already coached football for fifteen years when Russell was born. But their chemistry defies age. Their reflection of each other is a quintessential example of an elite quarterback-head coach relationship in today's NFL.

This was never more apparent than in their Super Bowl XLIX loss to New England. The stupefying game where they were close to the winning score in the final seconds and then Wilson was intercepted by Patriots cornerback Malcolm Butler.

Adversity in the NFL can destroy bonds. It can also strengthen them. It can reveal just how much symmetry exits between a quarterback and his head coach. Because after that play, Wilson walked to the sideline directly in front of Carroll. No words were exchanged.

Carroll said that night: "We just looked at each other trying to realize the gravity of what we just witnessed."

This is how Carroll describes it now: "Before I even looked up, a flash of an instant, I sensed a real clarity for me what that moment was. There was nothing hopeful. Just a couple of snaps left. A real test. Here comes Russell. He knows there was nothing that could be said. We have talked extensively about it since. Real. This is the real test. We practiced that a ton. That's why we threw it. Next play would have been a run. We were going to use all four plays.

"But there was also the Super Bowl win. We were winning big early but Russell did not celebrate in that game early. He stayed right on it. He kept telling everyone to focus. Our classic way. But I think I might have had a little more fun with it. He was actually doing the job better than me."

Russell Wilson and Pete Carroll look back and see how things have blown by so fast. The future for both optimists looks good. This is what they preach. This is who they are.

"I really look forward to seeing how Russell's game grows," Carroll said. "He is five years old in the NFL compared to guys who did it a long time, like Peyton and Brady and Roethlisberger.

This [2017] season will be his sixth season. Some of those guys have ten years on him. The maturity and the command, I look forward to that. And it will all naturally take place. It will happen. I think about how far we have already come. He still wants it so badly. He can be one of the real greats."

* * *

When the NFL head coach and his young quarterback are at odds, it is not insurmountable. In certain instances in NFL history, teams have thrived in that situation. But often it leads to losing and chaos. And sometimes a toxic split.

Quarterback Jim McMahon and his 1985 Super Bowl shuffling Chicago Bears were a raucous team led by a rowdy quarterback. And his head coach, Mike Ditka, was equally boisterous.

McMahon was Chicago's first-round pick, No. 5 overall, in 1982. The Bears were convinced he would become their franchise quarterback and from 1982 through 1988 he was indeed that. But he and Ditka disagreed and squabbled in both private and public. McMahon believes his Bears would have won more Super Bowls with a better approach from Ditka.

In a 2015 inteview with Comcast SportsNet's *Inside Look*, McMahon was blunt in his description: "I would've loved to have played with Mike, he was a great football player. And had he ever been in my huddle he would have understood me, I think. We would have gotten along better as players. I think we just got tired of beating each other up and that takes a toll after a while. Our offense was so predicatable. Unless I changed the play, everybody knew what we were going to run. Things just caught up to us."

Things were toxic from the start between then Oakland Raiders head coach Lane Kiffin and rookie quarterback JaMarcus Russell in 2007. Russell was Oakland's and the draft's No. 1 pick. Kiffin did not want him. Then Raiders owner Al Davis forced the union. The connection had no chance and fizzled after two seasons when Kiffin was fired. The Raiders booted Russell the following season. The Robert Griffin III-Jay Gruden link in Washington followed a similar path for the quarterback. Gruden arrived in 2014 as head coach and inherited Griffin. After one season as the starter, Griffin did not take a snap the following season and afterward was jettisoned. It was clearly an oil-water relationship.

Few such relationships can match the sudden snap of the one between Houston Texans head coach Bill O'Brien and quarterback Brock Osweiler. On March 9, 2016, the Texans made a splashy, expensive, brazen free agent move for Osweiler. On March 9, 2017, Osweiler was traded to the Cleveland Browns.

The deal was for four years, $72 million with $37 million guaranteed. By Week 15, Osweiler was benched. By season's end, reports surfaced that the head coach and quarterback had a physical confrontation in the locker room during halftime in Week 17 at the Tennessee Titans.[4] Pure oil and water.

It has not always been smooth in Green Bay between head coach Mike McCarthy and quarterback Aaron Rodgers. Total agreement will probably never happen. But that's OK, both say. They have described their conflict as "good." Rodgers wants to take more chances. McCarthy wants him to run the offense. Rodgers occasionally disagrees with the play calls. McCarthy wants him to run the offense. Thus far, through 10 seasons and

---

4. The Texans were down 14–0 at halftime, and lost the game 24–17.

a Super Bowl XLV championship, they have created shared and winning ground.

A common thread in most of these instances is that young quarterbacks suffered in their growth and grooming and in their NFL experience from fractured and sometimes bitter relationships with their head coaches. The quarterback in some instances created the issues with his play and attitude. In others he was the victim of a misguided, bitter approach by his head coach.

The 2017 season will provide more intriguing head coach-quarterback drama.

Chief among them is how head coach Andy Reid and quarterback Alex Smith adapt in their fifth season together in Kansas City, with rookie franchise quarterback Patrick Mahomes in the fold and unabashedly Smith's replacement.

Smith has lived this testy scenario before.

He was the 2005 draft's No. 1 overall pick by San Franciso, and in his first six 49ers seasons worked with a different offensive coordinator each year. In 2011, he connected with head coach Jim Harbaugh and led the 49ers to a 13–3 record, a playoff victory, and into the NFC Championship game. The following season he was 6–2 when a concussion sidelined him. He was replaced by younger quarterback Colin Kaepernick and never regained his job. Kaepernick led the 49ers to the Super Bowl and Smith was traded to the Chiefs soon afterward.

The following season, Smith won his first nine games as a Chief. He led them to the playoffs in that 2013 season, the Chiefs' first playoff appearance since 1994. He became a two-time Pro Bowl quarterback and produced a 41–20 record in his four seasons as Chiefs starter. He won . . . but he apparently did not win enough. Reid and the Chiefs reached for Mahomes in the 2017 draft, and it is only a matter of time before Mahomes supplants Smith. It could be in the 2017 season. It likely will be no later than the following season.

Smith enters the 2017 season with his eyes wide open but with his heart, surely, initially crushed. He expects that no matter what happens, he and the Chiefs have a high-road way of doing things. He does not forsee the situation getting ugly.

But his development as a franchise quarterback took so many turns from the moment he entered the league that lingering frustration has built. Just when he thought he had found a solid home, the floor could possibly be caving in. How this all manifests among the Chiefs is unknown. All we can do is stay tuned.

"You've got to go out there and do your deal," Smith said. "We all have to. Whether or not we drafted Patrick [Mahomes], it doesn't change that, right? If you're not good enough and didn't get it done, you're not going to be around long. That's just our culture. I know it. That's the nature of the position."

Rookie quarterbacks must realize this facet of their careers, this element of their lives from the second they step into the league. Their relationship with their head coach is vital. The patience they are granted varies from team to team, but the expiration of that patience for each one ticks steadily. Every snap, every moment counts.

Can this franchise quarterback get us to the Super Bowl? Can he win it all? That is the stark, final measurement of a franchise quarterback. It is one teams continually ask themselves, even during the process.

His leadership, his communication, and his relationship with his head coach are factors that heavily sway all answers.

Chapter 4

A BORN LEADER: DAK ATTACK

Dak Prescott says moving from backup quarterback to starter has been a constant in his football experience. He says being a biracial man helped him learn to move easily among races in his locker rooms. He says losing his mother, Peggy, to cancer in 2013 while he was at Mississippi State has molded a steel-like nature within him.

He insists that his preparation has always matched his desire. He is confident that when the games get bigger, he gets stronger. He has no doubts that he was born to lead.

The Dallas Cowboys have become quickly convinced of that, too.

All of the Cowboys proclaim that Dak Prescott is a born leader. This moment helped stir the journey that has made the Cowboys believers.

It was the Cowboys' third preseason game of 2016, and a frolicking affair was unfolding at the Seattle Seahawks' Century-Link Field. It was the Cowboys' principal dress rehearsal for the regular season, so starters were expected to play well into the third quarter.

That included quarterback Tony Romo, who planned to commence his 10th straight Cowboys season as their opening day starter. The season prior he had broken his clavicle and managed only four starts, 121 pass attempts, 5 touchdown passes, and 7 interceptions. That led Dallas to a paltry 4–12 season-long splat where they switched starting quarterbacks four times.[1]

This Seattle game, this Dallas 2016 season, was healing time for Romo. It was late-career redemption. A brawny offensive line and flexible receivers were in place, and breezy rookie running back Ezekiel Elliott had surfaced to buttress everything around Romo. This veteran quarterback, a four-time Pro Bowler, anticipated his finest football.

But three plays in at Seattle, Romo scrambled, Seattle defensive end Cliff Avril mauled him, and Romo lay sprawled out on the turf.

"You could instantly tell that Tony was out of that game and that it meant more than just out," Cowboys offensive coordinator Scott Linehan said of Romo's fractured back. "I remember the look on the sideline, the faces of the coaches and the players. There was shock. There was concern. That is, with everybody but Dak Prescott. I turned to Dak and said, 'Warm up.' He looked at me and said, 'OK.' He had a look on his face like, 'OK, here is my chance.'

"Here was our franchise quarterback injured and ready to go to the locker room, and Dak was able to calm everything down.

---

1. Tony Romo (3–1), Brandon Weeden (0–3), Matt Cassel (1–6), and Kellen Moore (0–2).

He played some of his best football all year in that game, including the regular season. He put to rest right there if we were going to need to go out and get a veteran quarterback to become the starter for the regular season. He wasn't the most decorated recruit at Mississippi State; he had to get there and prove it.[2] He was a fourth-round pick for us; he had to prove it.[3] It's funny, every time he has played, from high school to college to the pros, he has had to come in and replace someone injured that everyone was counting on. He's like the Lone Ranger. Maybe that's what God chose for him to do, be the guy that saves seasons, be the Plan B when Plan A is gone. Maybe that will be his legacy one day: 'Dak, the guy who always saved us.'"

* * *

Prescott had started the first preseason game and completed 10 of 12 passes for 139 yards and two touchdowns at the LA Coliseum, dwarfing the quarterback drafted 134 spots higher, the Rams' Jared Goff, the No. 1 overall pick of the 2016 NFL Draft. Prescott rolled onward against Seattle and in following Cowboys practices. He had started the season as the No. 3 quarterback on the Dallas depth chart, but backup Kellen Moore had been lost four days into training camp due to a broken leg. Moore out. Romo out. Dallas turned to Prescott to save its season.

He did more than that.

---

2. Prescott was the third player drafted from Mississippi State, with DT Chris Jones (KC Chiefs, 2-37) and CB Will Redmond (SF 49ers, 3-68) being picked before him.
3. He was the eighth of fifteen quarterbacks drafted in 2016.

Dallas finished with an NFC-best 13–3 record, tying a franchise record. Prescott threw 25 touchdown passes and 4 interceptions. He set a league record for most pass attempts (176) to start a career without an interception, and later in the season threw another 171 consecutive passes without an interception. His 67.7 pass completion percentage set a league rookie record. His 88.9 pass completion percentage against the Tampa Bay Buccaneers on December 18 set a rookie single-game record. He was named the AP Offensive Rookie of the Year and earned Pro Bowl honors.

"It was a good experience, something that in my mind is just a start, not a big accomplishment," Prescott said.

No, it was a spectacular start. A spectacular accomplishment. A spectacular season—even without a Super Bowl championship.

In a league where teams gamble on starting rookie quarterbacks and often see them crash, Prescott took the gamble out of it with a historic and remarkable spell.

Consider that since the league moved to a 16-game schedule in 1978, only eighteen quarterbacks started all 16 games in their rookie season. Besides Prescott, only Matt Ryan, Joe Flacco, Andrew Luck, Andy Dalton, and Russell Wilson from that group pushed their teams into the playoffs. None won a division title in doing so, as Prescott did. And consider that Cowboys Hall of Fame quarterback Troy Aikman threw 18 interceptions in his rookie season in 1989 and finished 0–11 as a starter.

Prescott lost his Dallas debut versus the Giants, and then won 11 straight.

Seventeen games, one season into his career, Prescott is already viewed by Dallas as its franchise quarterback. Romo saw it, too, choosing to retire after the season in early April and later move into a TV broadcasting career. If Prescott proves that he's the future, then Dallas owner Jerry Jones has found three franchise quarterbacks during his twenty-eight-year tenure that cover remarkable spectrums: Aikman was the 1989 draft's No. 1 overall pick, Romo was a 2003 undrafted free agent signee, and Prescott was a 2016 mid-round draft pick.

Prescott navigated reservations and bruises from scouts. He was equipped when Romo buckled. He overcame losing his first pro game and the continuous doubt which circled around him. He remained humble when the winning streak raged and during the constant harangue about Romo's potential return. Even in the home playoff loss to the Green Bay Packers, he completed 24 of 38 passes for 302 yards with three touchdown passes and an interception.

"He was everything that you could dream about if you had a make-believe situation on a rookie quarterback," Jones said. "He played in a veteran way. He made those kinds of decisions. He kept steady. He never, as long as he had the opportunity, equivocated as far as his decisions and playing winning football."

* * *

During the 2015 Cowboys season, Scott Linehan kept flipping on his TV and catching SEC games where Mississippi State quarterback Dak Prescott was showing poise and sturdiness—whether he was throwing touchdown passes or getting pummeled in the pocket. That stuck with Linehan.

"That's what life in the NFL is all about, getting knocked down and getting up and being able to shake things off might be the greatest strength you need," Linehan said. "Especially at quarterback."

Later, Linehan got his hands on copies of Prescott's game video from an end zone view and began getting a feel for him "running a football team like a point guard," with ability to distribute the ball and with a calming effect. His college games were fast, it was often helter-skelter, but Prescott seemed to be playing at a pace of his own, a controlled speed.

It was Linehan who told Jones in the Cowboys 2016 draft process, "Jerry, I think I can work with this guy."

That kind of Dallas open conversation and communication between the offensive coordinator and the owner/GM served Dallas well.

The Dallas coaches met Prescott in late January at the 2016 Senior Bowl in Mobile, Alabama. He was on the opposing team but, for a day, the players switched teams, and the Dallas coaches gained the chance to work with him directly. He simply stood out, they said. "A natural, genuine, unique glow about him—a natural leader," they wrote in their Senior Bowl reports.

Wade Wilson, the Cowboys quarterbacks coach, returned from Prescott's pro day workouts later in March impressed. Dallas decided they wanted Prescott in their building for an even closer look in early April. Between his pro day and that visit, Prescott was cited for DUI near his Mississippi State campus. Though the charges were later dropped in July, it clearly was a factor in him lasting until the fourth round of the late-April NFL draft.

"He came in here and won the head coach over," Linehan said of Dallas coach Jason Garrett. "It was as good an interview as I've seen. We put him through the wringer and he didn't try to deny anything, was genuine about his mistake, and said the lesson was learned and he was determined. Sometimes when you get guys in situations like that you can literally see the wheels spinning as they try to put a story together, but this was not the case. It was what you wanted to hear, accountability. Nobody's perfect. Can you learn and be inspired? Well, that's something that really held true in the entire first year we had him."

The Cowboys realize they were lucky to get Dak Prescott in the fourth round, the 135th pick. That is the draft business; those occasions where a player will slide into the middle rounds because of something he has done or something other teams missed. In some teams' analysis, Prescott was not just a gamble to start as a rookie quarterback, he was a gamble to even draft. If he is going to get a DUI in the middle of his NFL scouting process and so close to the draft, some teams pondered, then why bother?

For Dallas, more luck arose.

They tried to trade up in the 2016 draft to select either quarterback Paxton Lynch or Connor Cook. Both attempts failed. But they kept their eyes on Prescott. The Dallas offensive coaches had placed a gold star by his name. Thus, the draft pick was made and neither the Cowboys, nor Prescott thus far, regret it.

Thrust into the starting role, Dallas planned to make it work by everyone—the coaches, the players, the entire franchise—doing more around their rookie quarterback. Prescott made it work by paying attention. He mastered his chance to overcome his DUI blunder. He embraced Dallas and was ready—physically and emotionally—when Romo was lost. He would prove to all he had the mindset for it. "The blood pressure for it," Linehan likes to say.

"There is no quarterback I have been around in my Dallas ownership years who prepares as meticulously and as hard as

Dak Prescott," Jones said. Troy Aikman agreed. "This is one of the traits that served him very well."

Even after his 20–19 debut loss against the Giants.

The Giants had made dramatic defensive changes via free agency, and the Cowboys say that Giants defensive coordinator Steve Spagnuolo is one of the toughest minds and schemers they face every year. Dallas expected Prescott to compete against great odds against the Giants and to bounce back against the Washington Redskins the following week. The fact that Prescott did so was the first winning step in his streak of 11 consecutive victories.

Had he lost that game, and Dallas started 0–2, does a winning streak still commence? Was the common theme and frequent assumption often floated correct: that Dallas could only hope that Prescott (or maybe even backup and former No. 5 overall pick Mark Sanchez) could manage a 4–4 record until Romo's return?

"That was a bunch of nonsense," Cowboys rookie running back Ezekiel Elliott said. "I mean, it was just preposterous to think that way. Dak and I talked about this all of the time even before the first game against the Giants and all the way through, that kind of stupid thinking and talk. When you have had success as a college football player, when you've played in big games and had success in football all of your life, there is no reason to believe that you just have to fit into a profile in the NFL. Rookie quarterback, rookie running back does not have to mean 4–4 to start the season. We just laughed at that when we kept hearing it. We are just not wired like that. Our thinking all along was to win them all. Dak never thought anything differently from that. He helped convince the entire team, the entire franchise, to think that way. Dak is a natural leader."

The Cowboys front office and coaches left the Washington game with a 1–1 record and thinking about Prescott, *He's got something*.

Over the next few weeks, the Dallas offense was massaged even more in sync with Prescott's skills, including a few added elements of the spread offense. The way Dallas saw it, Mississippi State's version of the spread offense incorporated several NFL elements. The way Dallas saw it, no college or pro offense runs the old-fashioned pro I-set formation every play. Dallas was not concerned about Prescott's spread offense background. Instead, the Cowboys focused on his versatility and leadership in that offense. Dallas created an operative blend for Prescott.

He created higher efficiency in accuracy, in his third-down plays, and in the red zone. He began to be more cautious in fringe areas when Dallas was in field goal range and protected those opportunities. Prescott began to share a working knowledge of NFL players with Dallas coaches, which impressed them. He was insightful in discussing defensive players he had already faced in college who were upcoming on the schedule, offering for example, "That's a bad man right there—he got me in college on this play, let me show you . . ." and the conversations would spin from there into attack plans and offensive personnel packages that would create answers.

Eyebrows around the league were raised when the Cincinnati Bengals traveled to Dallas for a Week 5 match-up on October 9. Dallas strangled them early with a 28–0 blitz and won, 28–14. Linehan had been telling Prescott that, in his first season as an NFL head coach in 2006 with the St. Louis Rams, he was amazed at how fast the games went. He told Prescott those games would be over, yet it felt like halftime. It was a reminder for Prescott to treat every possession with care. In this game against Cincinnati, Prescott exhibited that kind of control.

His efficiency impressed his head coach, Garrett, who said: "It's a challenge for every quarterback. If you think about it, you get the ball 60 to 70 plays a game, the ball is in your hands, and everybody's coming to get it. You might drop back 25 to 30 times and you have to be a great decision-maker. You have to understand what the offense is trying to do, what the defense is trying to do, and how it all fits together in a short period of time. He's done a really good job processing things. Clearly his experience in college has helped him, but I believe his preparation is off the charts. He's just ready. He understands what we're asking him to do. He sees how it fits together and what the defense is trying to do and he's a poised, composed athlete. He's certainly plenty talented. The other part of it, too, is that he learns from his experiences. He doesn't make the same mistakes over and over again. He takes his practice play into the game and I just think he's getting better and better."

It was also after that victory against Cincinnati, which improved Dallas to a 4–1 record, that Jones said the following: "Do we think Dak Prescott can win more regular season games and have a strong regular season? Yes, we do. Do we think Tony Romo gives us the best chance to win a Super Bowl? Yes, we do. Tony is going to be the starter when he's healthy and ready."

Prescott chimed in: "This is Tony Romo's team."

And it was . . . until it wasn't.

Because Dak Prescott won the next week at hallowed Lambeau Field against the Green Bay Packers. And the next two weeks against the Philadelphia Eagles and Cleveland Browns. The Cowboys were impressed with how Prescott handled the Lambeau experience. No awe. Just play. Just win.

They were 7–1 and headed for a Week 10 game against the Pittsburgh Steelers on November 13.

Romo was ready, but Prescott was soaring. Romo was told by Garrett that week that not only would Prescott start against the Steelers but that he was the starter for the remainder of the season. Linehan told Prescott the same thing. Romo wanted to compete for the job. Romo wanted to play. It was a definitive "no" from the Dallas hierarchy. Jones and his son, Stephen, the team's president, met with Romo.

"There is something about holding the hot hand that you just can't ignore," Stephen Jones said. "Tony had told me once he got hurt that he thought we were in way better position than the year before, that we had a backup in Dak who could win some games. He thought Dak could go at least 4–4. He said, 'If he winds up winning them all, changing, going back to me, would be hard to do . . . but we'll cross that river when it happens.'"

Prescott had not won them all—but he had won 7 of 8 and all in a row. Romo wanted to play. Romo was ready. But Prescott was now entrenched.

"It's just kind of how it evolved," Stephen Jones said. "Dak was able to walk in and check all of the boxes. It's not normal for a rookie quarterback to pull that off. He's confident. He has a tremendous set of leadership skills. He showed it from the first day he walked into the building. He has that 'it' factor that is so hard to find. He's got the people skills. He's got the quarterback skills."

Prescott was not Plan B anymore. He was Plan A. He won in striking fashion at Pittsburgh, 35–31. Soon afterward, Romo conducted a conceding news conference to Prescott. He acknowledged the Cowboys were now Prescott's team. The Dallas season from that moment forward morphed into league-wide curiosity over this rookie starting quarterback's march to the playoffs and possibly the Super Bowl.

Romo began the week after the Pittsburgh game with an emotional news conference where he, essentially, passed the torch to Prescott. He did it with grace. He did it in anguish. But throughout the season, he kept by the rookie's side.

* * *

The ingredients were there for Prescott to become distracted. The Romo fuss had lingered. His early success could have boosted his ego out of whack.

And when you are the winning starting quarterback of the Dallas Cowboys, you are the star of the city. You are an instant icon of the state. The Cowboys' national and global reach is formidable. Prescott, a rookie, could have easily gotten caught up. Blinded. Lost in his own revelry.

Linehan told Prescott to not let all he heard and read about the Romo situation distract him. He challenged him to stay on course.

He answered: "Coach, the things I've been through in my life, some of those were a distraction. This is not."

Linehan recalled: "He said it like an old, wise man."

He beat the Baltimore Ravens and the Washington Redskins. He won at the Minnesota Vikings. Then he lost 10–7 at the Giants. The Cowboys say inclement weather was a problem for them in that game. And the Giants were a problem again, too. Neither did the Cowboys handle well.

"We had won 11 in a row, lost a game, and now all of a sudden again the sky was falling," Linehan said. "Dak and I knew that was not the case. He just had to get right back on that horse. We were playing Tampa Bay next. They have a super-fast defense. We did not want to find out how much things could turn if we lost two in a row. I met with Dak and told him I would be pissed off if he did not come back and complete 80 percent against Tampa Bay. And he went out there and completed 32 of 35 passes for 88.9 percent! It's hard to do that throwing just against air. The ball rarely touched the ground."

Dallas won that game, 26–20, and then crushed Detroit the following week, 42–21. The Cowboys finished the regular season with a 27–13 loss at Philadelphia—Prescott was removed as precaution after the second drive of the game—before taking a bye week for the playoffs. On January 15, 2017, Prescott made his playoff debut. This time the Packers were on his home turf, AT&T Stadium.

"We went into that game very confident," Dallas star receiver Dez Bryant said. "And one of the reasons for that was because what Dak had done all year. We were blessed to have Tony Romo as our quarterback. And when he got hurt, we were blessed again with a guy like Dak. I love the guy. There are very few people that reach out and touch a team like he can. Touch a soul. Touch your soul. And then he's smart and he makes the right plays. He's special. I love the guy."

The Dallas playoff crowd was amped, but Green Bay quarterback Aaron Rodgers was surgical. He led the Packers to a fast start. Prescott was challenged once again to match it—which he did. He twice led the Cowboys to fourth quarter ties. Green Bay finally won it, 34–31, on a field goal with three seconds left.

Prescott told the Dallas coaches the day after: "I'm at this office and I can't believe the season is over. I expected to be in here preparing for the NFC Championship game. Where do

I go? What do I do? I set the bar high for my rookie year. We didn't get anywhere close to what I set out to do."

Once again, Prescott was displaying his "old soul."

He told them he wanted to work with his teammates during the offseason while he himself developed. He said he wanted to evaluate how the Cowboys' returning players and the new ones yet to come would fit with him and he with them. He was thinking like a franchise quarterback.

And all season long, he inspired the players around him.

He explained in an interview with *USA Today* before the playoffs how his upbringing colors his communication with teammates:

> I grew up in Haughton, Louisiana. I go to my white grandparents' house and then I cross the railroad tracks and hang out with my black grandma. We have English teachers on my white side. My grandpa is a principal. And then you go to the other side and people have been in jail. I was put in all those different situations. I've been in situations where I was the only black guy. We're in a time now where nobody wants to see that. But it still happens. Depending on where you come from, it happens. To be able to wipe that clean and see and live both sides, it's just who I am. Being mixed allows me to connect with everyone.
>
> Being biracial and being from the country, I can talk to guys like [offensive linemen] Travis Frederick from Wisconsin and Doug Free from Wisconsin. And then I can go over and talk to Dez Bryant. I mean, think about the two different standpoints you need to have a

real conversation with both, to really understand what they've been through. I don't think many can do it. For me, it's not hard. I'm blessed because it's natural.

* * *

Dak Prescott's rookie season was full of support, including an offensive cast that was superior at most positions by NFL standards. Especially his offensive line, routinely considered the best in the NFL—a line that is like a romping convoy in cleats.

But NFL coaching legend Paul Brown used to always say, "It is one thing to have good players, and a totally different thing to get good players to play good." Prescott, to rise, to elevate Dallas, was still required to display a mindset, a blood pressure, a near-perfect poise no matter what surrounded him.

Garrett was stunned by Prescott's season, explaining: "I have never seen a rookie quarterback handle everything as well as he did. I have never seen a rookie quarterback do what he was able to do. I close my eyes and I go back to that first time we saw him in rookie minicamp and how he came in and how he handled himself in meetings, in walk-throughs, out on the practice field. He's always prepared, he's always ready for any situation, he's got great poise and composure. He has great confidence in himself and he's able to transfer that confidence to the people around him. He has unique leadership skills that people respond to."

There was no "C" on his jersey for captain during his rookie season, but his Dallas teammates will tell you that Prescott led them, inspired them in profound ways. Even before Romo was finally determined the backup, Prescott took control of the Cowboys in a way few individual players have in franchise history.

He lived it.

He embraced it.

"Sometimes I almost pinched myself when I was talking to him because it did not feel like I was talking to a twenty-three-year-old," Linehan said. "We didn't even have him on the team last year for the whole offseason, so, entering his second year, that will make a difference."

Linehan and Garrett will tell Prescott that the league will study him with intensity and that he must study himself and the league with even more intensity. Surprising elements from his rookie season he must now anticipate. What was his worst play? Why? What adjustments will he make? What is he going to do to make sure his rookie season was not a fluke? How will he fight being complacent about the 13–3 record and making the playoffs? Find answers, the Dallas coaches say they will tell him.

Pay attention.

Prescott will remind them that he does not need reminding. That he is paying attention and always has—it's his DNA. The game is where he finds peace. The game is his refuge. Football is his passion. And so are the Cowboys.

"I've never seen any player that can talk to anyone in such a way as he does," Linehan said. "It is an aura, a glow that makes you feel good being around him. He makes people feel important. He makes teammates play harder for him. This was the most unique season that I have ever been a part of. People say leaders are not born, they can be created. I disagree. It is an innate thing. Dak Prescott is a born leader."

* * *

A couple of days in early April 2017 after Romo retired, he and Prescott exchanged a few text messages. Each thanked the other for their friendship. Romo was heading to the broadcast booth and Prescott was even more synced with the trademark star of Dallas. The Cowboys, truly, were his team now.

"All of the times during the season where I said it was Tony's team, I meant it, but I also thought it was a job I had earned, so, it was a little of both," Prescott said. "I needed to say that during the process while really feeling it was *our* team. We all were Dallas Cowboys, whatever role we played. But Tony had fourteen years in the NFL and with the team. It didn't hurt me to go along with the questions the media was asking and how they might have been hoping I would speak against him. I wasn't going to let that happen."

Prescott said he knew his DUI before he was drafted hurt him with some NFL teams, but he committed to fixing it as best he could in team draft interviews, especially in the one with Dallas.

"I accepted it," Prescott said. "How was I going to get them to accept it? I did not feel I was guilty. I had put myself in a bad situation with friends, I was not drunk in my mind, but by the law, the law said I was. I took the responsibility when I talked with the Dallas organization. I told them my story straight. They grilled me on it. But I promised them this: I don't make the same mistakes in life. I earned my degree in psychology. I use the mental side to put a chip on my shoulder. I promised them moving forward I would help anybody, especially a teammate, in that situation. I was very grateful when it was later tossed out, well before the season, so my focus could be on the Cowboys.

"From high school to college, you are taught as a quarterback you are one play away from getting in there, and in both of those instances that is exactly what happened, the starter got hurt and boom! I'm in. So, when it happened with Tony, I just ran with it. I know how to put myself in position to be successful. I've had many tests. None was tougher than when I lost my mom to colon cancer in November 2013. I learned how not to stress and overthink things. The DUI, losing my mom, Tony getting hurt and being tossed in, being down 20-something points in a play-off game? I'm not a person who runs from adversity. I graduated from high school early. I earned my masters degree in psychology at twenty-two. I became a starter as a rookie. I've always done things early. I've always hung out with people older than me. I know I'm young, but I've lived. I have some knowledge in life."

He describes the game of football as his vehicle for inner peace.

"When I am in a game, or even in practice, the rest just goes away. It's just football. It's what I live to do. I feel no stress. I feel no DUI. I feel no tragedy. The game gives me peace. I'm free. I just play the game."

This helped account for his cool during his rookie season. As drama and pressure swirled around him, he remained collected off the field and in the pocket.

He remembers those conversations with fellow rookie Ezekiel Elliott as they prepared for the 2016 season. The insistence that 4–4 would not do.

"It's just a simple fact in life, and, really, I just don't know how any human being can go into any game or any job and think, *If I just do it average, I will do well.* If you think that way, you will never be great. I don't care if you are a rookie or a ten-year guy in the NFL. A record of 4–4 is not good. That turns into 8–8 and no playoffs. The Cowboys' expectations are greater. Mine are greater."

Here are the moments from his extraordinary rookie season that he said he will never forget:

- The Week 1 start and loss to the Giants: "We lost and then win 11 in a row. If we had won that one, there is no telling what our record would have been for the season. I think the whole season would have been even better."
- The Week 2 start and victory over Washington: "My first win. There was a lot that went down in that game that gave me even more confidence."
- The game-winning touchdown pass in overtime to tight end Jason Witten in Week 8: "It was my first score to him. And it was in a game where he set a record for most consecutive Cowboys starts. A lot of emotion went into that."
- His time before the Week 10 game against Pittsburgh: "Tony was ready to come back. We were 7–1. Things had been building. If they did pull me, I wasn't going to change. Coach Linehan pulled me off to the side. It was the Monday or Tuesday of that week. It was early. He said, 'You are the quarterback, and we are riding with you.' I already felt that way. I was ready for anything. It didn't change the way I worked or the way I played."
- The Week 12 Thanksgiving Day victory over Washington: "I grew up watching the Dallas Thanksgiving game for many years. Zeke and I shared that TV game trophy. I wish it had been an actual turkey leg like they did in the old days. I could see Zeke and I chomping on that. It would have been fun."
- The Week 15 victory over Tampa Bay: "That was after the second Giants loss. There were a lot of people talking after the Giants loss. People had this and that to say about me and

about the team. I played some of the best of the season to try to fix that. And it helped in the next week when we won a Monday night game against Detroit. Those were really big games to quiet down some noise." The playoff loss to Green Bay: "We didn't win. We fought back. We didn't win."

Prescott's Louisiana hometown is a three-hour drive from Dallas. He grew up a Cowboys fan. Along with his rookie production, his greatest accomplishment was duplicating the deep affection and trust that the Cowboys players and franchise had for Romo. In every nook and corner of the locker room, in every office in the Cowboys complex, Prescott was open, displayed humanity, and exuded a confident, sometimes bold, sometimes hushed assurance. Romo did that beautifully during his time in Dallas. Prescott is doing it, too.

The day after Romo retired, Prescott was at the complex training, preparing for the 2017 season.

"Well, this is how games are won," he said immediately after his workout session. "They give you a training regimen for the offseason and I combine it with one of my own that I've always used and that I believe in. I just left a workout that in my mind just won a game. I do everything I can when I get to Sundays where I can't go back and pinpoint a reason or think of a workout or a practice that I wish I had done differently or worked harder. There are no excuses for not getting that right. This is the work you do to get that.

"I just want to be a great player. A leader. Let my passion for the game show. Make my teammates and coaches better. Win."

And keep seizing his "peace" in the game.

* * *

Prescott and the Cowboys in mid-June conducted their final mandatory camp at the team's sprawling, sparkling facility, The Star in Frisco, Texas. It was a reminder for Prescott that this off-season work was unlike that of his rookie year. This time he was the starter gaining the majority of reps. He was the starter sharpening his mental game as much as his physical one. He was the anointed franchise quarterback helping to set the tone on how the Cowboys work and the view on exactly where they are going.

All in the organization expect his leadership to flourish in training camp, the preseason, and into the 2017 regular season.

His confidence in this camp was compelling.

"I think confidence in the NFL is one of the most underrated traits you can have," Prescott said. "Everybody is capable at this level. But do you really believe you can do it?"

Prescott cultivates that characteristic among the Cowboys.

This scene during that mid-June camp revealed the type of powerful examples he sets while all eyes are on him.

Raymond "Ray Ray" Melgarejo was at that Cowboys camp from the Make-A-Wish Foundation. Melgarejo, age nine, a California kid, had a brain tumor removed from the back of his head. It was discovered while he was putting on his football helmet. His family says that football saved his life.

Prescott connected with the boy in a dynamic way. He invited him onto the practice field. He instructed him to deliver a hand-off to Ezekiel Elliott. Prescott allowed Malgarejo to stand next to him during his news conference with the media. He advised him on confidence.

He inspired him.

He made a wish come true in a veritable, tolerant, earnest way with everyone watching.

"This is the thing we're talking about that Dak has that you can't teach, you can't create, it's just there," teammate Jason Witten said. "It's natural. People feel better around Dak. They believe. He's got the talent. But he's got this thing that matters just as much.

"There is a hunger here for a championship that we feel every day. Every conversation that I have every day with Jerry [Jones], I feel it rising from the pit of his stomach. It's just there. It's real. And Dak wants it as much as any of us. You just have to have that in your quarterback in this league to have any chance. We do."

Chapter 5

SHATTERED DREAMS

A highly drafted NFL quarterback enters the league with glitz and glee. The hope, on all fronts, is that he is a franchise quarterback. The desire is he will become the face of the team. The plan is he will be a dazzling light of the city and organization.

NFL history is littered with illustrations where a young quarterback's fast start faded into shattered dreams. It is filled with other instances where he quickly crashed. The ugly characterization afterward is he's a flop. The nastiest is he's a bust.

That label—bust—cascades a lasting sting for the quarterback and the franchise. He can find it taxing to escape this brutal narrative. It can become a lifetime tag more utilized than his actual name.

The factors for his demise, however, are often complex.

"Potential can be the best thing said about a young quarterback, and it can also be the worst," Green Bay Packers head coach Mike McCarthy said. "The good young quarterbacks go through a process where they learn how to do things and how to deal with high expectations. When you find a starting quarterback in this league who has lasted ten or more years, I don't think that guy gets enough credit for how elite he is. That is a very rare group of men. But I can't stress it enough: for the ones that struggle, fit is important, too."[1]

Rookie quarterbacks routinely struggle with the leap from college offenses and defenses to NFL levels of both. The action around them is faster—a blur—and the athletes they compete with and against are all premium. A popular NFL adage describes it this way: college is like learning beginners Spanish and the NFL is like being dropped into the middle of Mexico City expected to speak it fluently.

It is a mammoth adjustment.

"They are used to throwing into more wide open areas and they get to our level where windows are tighter and that is a big struggle," Jacksonville Jaguars head coach Doug Marrone said. "The speed of NFL defenses leads to rookie quarterbacks struggling with accuracy. It's that way for veteran quarterbacks a lot, too, but with rookies, it can be so significant."

Whether a rookie franchise quarterback initially sits or starts, the pressure on him and his head coach boils.

"Say you get picked in the top five, sometimes even the first round. The expectation level is so high to be great right away," Tony Dungy said. "And even though there are Hall of Fame quarterbacks who were not great early, that expectation still exists. You have got to, as a head coach, have a strong organization behind you. We've seen coaches get fired in the middle of the process of working with a rookie franchise quarterback. The fear of being fired by these

---

1. Of the 32 starting quarterbacks in 2016, ten had been in the league for 10+ years, with five still with their original drafted team (Brady, Roethlisberger, Rivers, Manning, and Rodgers).

coaches while working with the new franchise guy is real. It colors their decisions. The fear of being fired during this process really needs to be taken off the table with frank discussions or at least with an understanding of what the organization expects for that season and beyond. Otherwise, the whole thing is clouded waters."

Jon Gruden adds: "Some of these quarterbacks labeled busts were put into horrible situations. The coaching and the systems were not good."

It is a raging storm.

The rookie franchise quarterback labeled a bust might have entered with lackluster work ethic and a pitiful, pious attitude— he walked through the door thinking "Diva." He might have entered a situation where the infighting between coach, management, and ownership was toxic. His tutoring might have been poor. The talent around him poorer. The locker room environment a mess. How to handle his big money, how to deal with his external pressures immense.

The result: nightmarish.

The conclusion: a bust. Shattered dreams.

"When you consider the guys called busts in NFL history, I do know that most of the time it wasn't about talent, but I don't know if they were driven people," said retired coach Mike Martz, designer of the St. Louis Rams "Greatest Show On Turf" offense that won Super Bowl XXXIV. Martz began coaching high school in 1973, college in 1975, and displayed a proficient offensive mind during his NFL coaching career that spanned from 1992 through 2011.

"The quarterback has to be the most competitive person on the team," Martz said. "And for those guys called busts, there was something missing there. Sometimes they were tough enough and sometimes they said the right things, but they didn't have the perseverance and tenacity to see things through. When things go bad, the head coach and the quarterback are the first people under fire. That quarterback has to be a tough dude. It's also worth asking who gets them? What are they doing with them? There are good people out there, good offensive coaches in the NFL—just not enough of them."

* * *

The last twenty-six years of NFL rookie franchise quarterbacks whose dreams were shattered, who crashed and were soon banished by their initial franchises offers a gloomy portrait. How can something so right go so wrong so fast?

In fact, for four straight seasons (1991–94), a quarterback was taken in the first round with expectations of greatness. They all failed.

> Todd Marinovich was the then Los Angeles Raiders' first round pick in 1991, at No. 24. He was an artistic lefty passer who the Raiders hoped would emulate the heroics of their Hall of Fame southpaw quarterback Ken Stabler. Marinovich lasted eight career games and threw only 8 touchdown passes and 9 interceptions. His father was an overbearing, taxing influence before and during his pro career. Drug use hampered his chances. He was out of the league after two Oakland seasons.

> David Klingler was the Cincinnati Bengals' first round pick in 1992, at No. 6. Klingler had performed the

unorthodox run-and-shoot offense in college at Houston and was good at it: In one game he threw 11 touchdown passes for 730 yards. His NFL play, however, was erratic. Shoulder surgeries slowed him. He was out of the league after the '97 season.

Rick Mirer was the Seattle Seahawks' first round pick in 1993, No. 2 overall. He started every game as a rookie and set the league ablaze, leading league rookie marks in attempts (486), completions (274), and passing yards (2,833). But he was out of Seattle by 1996, bounced to six other NFL teams, and finished with a 24–44 record as a starter. It seemed as though the bigger the games grew, the more he shrank.

Heath Shuler was the Washington Redskins' first round pick in 1994, No. 3 overall. He lasted three seasons in Washington before being traded to the New Orleans Saints. He lasted just five seasons in the league. He threw 15 touchdown passes and 33 interceptions in his career, and was never able to play fast enough or big enough to warrant Washington's huge investment.

Some people start bust conversations with Ryan Leaf.

Leaf has been vilified for a pro career that began with the San Diego Chargers in 1998. They made him the draft's No. 2 over-all pick, one selection behind Peyton Manning. Manning's lofty success and Leaf's messy struggles boosted criticisms of Leaf. So did the fact that the '98 pre-draft discussions about who was the better quarterback were frequent and tangible.

Leaf's work ethic was ridiculed. His quick temper was highlighted. His play was sloppy. He lasted only three seasons in San Diego and four in the league, though only playing in three of them due to injury. He dealt with drug issues that eventually led him to prison. He is now clean and works as a national spokesman for a recovering addicts group.

Leaf said he knows he set the Chargers organization back during his time there and that the setbacks lasted long after he was exiled. He said it was tough for him to live with the pain of his football pressure and failures, and primarily turned to mood-altering pills to live through the anxiety.

"I don't really want to talk about all the stuff from my football past," Leaf said. "I don't care much about other people's analysis of my football past. Right now, it is such a minimal part of my life. If anybody ever wants to talk to me about recovery and what to do, I'm happy to do that all day long."

He had this advice for future NFL rookie franchise quarterbacks: "I would say that just know that you are never the smartest guy in the room. Always learn more and reach to be better. That's the best advice I can give to rookie quarterbacks and also to every young player coming into the league. That's the best advice I would give to any person in any situation."

Tim Couch was the Cleveland Browns' first round pick in 1999, the No. 1 overall. He was part of an expansion team—the Browns' ballyhooed return to Cleveland.

He lasted five seasons in Cleveland, finishing with a 22–37 career record. He struggled running the offense consistently. He struggled with the Browns lack of continuity.

Couch and Akili Smith were in the same draft. Smith's story is mesmerizing.

Tony Dungy said of Smith's 1999 pre-draft workouts: "I have never seen a quarterback throw a more beautiful ball."

Akili Smith was the Cincinnati Bengals' first round pick in 1999, the No. 3 overall. His last Bengals season was in 2002. He went 3–14 as a starter.

Smith told the *San Diego Union Tribune* in a 2009 interview of soul-searching reflection: "There were times when the game was in slow motion and I was just out there executing. But for whatever reason, there was just no continuity."

Smith said he was in a bad environment. His coaches said he struggled processing information and analyzing defenses at game speed. They said he did not grasp the true nature of setting a leadership example in his job. Smith often sought refuge in his hometown of San Diego rather than sticking it out in Cincinnati.

"I stayed here in San Diego. That was probably one of my biggest problems," Smith said. "When I left Cincinnati I came to San Diego, that's when the partying began. I did things out of my character to try to get away from the misery in Cincinnati. I'm still paying for that. People today still judge me on what I did as far as the party scene was concerned."

The Bengals had endured eight consecutive seasons without a winning record before Smith arrived. The losing mounted after his arrival. He was booted, landed briefly in Green Bay and Tampa Bay, left the NFL for good in 2005, and then played in the Canadian Football League with the Calgary Stampeders. He left pro football for good in 2007.

"When you don't want to show up for work and everybody in the locker room is bickering and complaining and you're supposed to be the head of that team and you're hearing that continually, you're scared to throw an incomplete pass . . . it's tough. It's just so tough," Smith said of his Bengals time. "Everywhere I went, I felt it. You could just tell: I'm under a magnifying glass."

* * *

On September 8, 2002, the Houston Texans played their first NFL game. They were an expansion team hosting the Dallas Cowboys in a Texas battle of baby steps vs. tested ones.

It was also the debut of rookie franchise quarterback David Carr. Five months earlier, Carr was the first ever selection by the Texans, and the No. 1 overall pick in the draft out of Fresno State.

"It was big time," Carr said. "Coming from a small hometown city like Bakersfield and from a smaller college like Fresno State, it wasn't as much overwhelming as it was exciting. But what I also soon realized was the first time I did anything in the NFL was the first time the Houston Texans did anything in the NFL. And neither one of us really knew what we were doing. We were all trying to figure it out at the same time."

Tony Wyllie was the communications executive with the Texans, a role he now holds with the Washington Redskins. Wyllie said Carr "was the Houston Texans." Wyllie called him their present and their future.

"The expectations were very high, as well as the excitement," Wyllie recalled. "And everything was on his shoulders. He never said no to a media request. He never said no to a public appearance to help promote the Texans. David was totally adopted by that city. They knew his wife, his kids were born there. He became a son of Houston right away."

And is Carr still "a son" of Houston?

"No," Wyllie said. "Because he didn't win."

But he won that first-ever game against the Cowboys. A 19–10 victory that ignited the city.

"And ever since," Wyllie said, "we were always trying to recapture the magic of that night."

The Texans lost five straight games after that Dallas victory, and finished 4–12 in Carr's debut season. They were a 23–53 team in Carr's games.

The Texans blew it. He blew it.

The factors were multiple but a common thread—from the expansion draft choices to the way Carr was coached and handled to the way Carr studied and managed huge responsibilities— was that the Texans and Carr took missteps frequently along the way.

"We had seen expansion drafts in recent years in Carolina, Jacksonville, and Cleveland where the league felt it had given way too much in personnel from existing NFL teams to field those teams," Houston owner Bob McNair said. "You need the right blend of veteran and younger players, and we found right away that teams were not going to allow their good young players to leave. They wanted you to have their older players with higher salaries to clear their own salary cap."

Dom Capers was the head coach, Chris Palmer was the offensive coordinator, and Charley Casserly was the general manager. The Texans tried to build an offensive line for Carr, taking veteran left tackle Tony Boselli from the Jacksonville Jaguars with their first pick in the expansion draft. Their second pick was New York Jets tackle Ryan Young. Young was only twenty-six years old, but injuries limited him to only eight starts in that first

Texans season. Young opted to leave the Texans after only one season.

Boselli had been the second overall pick by the then-expansion Jaguars in 1995, was a 5-time Pro Bowler and 3-time First-Team All-Pro. He was thirty years old.

"Tony was injured, broke down, and never played a down for us," McNair said.

Thus, the Texans' initial goal and plan of protecting Carr with two prime offensive tackles soon fizzled.

"Building the offensive line became tough," said Carr, who in his first season was sacked 76 times, the most in league history for any rookie (by 20). "We'd have tryouts, get these players literally off the street, and on the next Sunday they would be playing for us. It wasn't a lack of effort. They were trying. We just didn't have the guys on the line and in too many other places to compete on a regular basis. There was a huge disconnect with the guys we had and what we were asked to do. We didn't have the personnel to fit Chris Palmer's system. He wanted to push the ball downfield and run longer routes. Others on the offensive staff wanted to get the ball out quicker and faster. I'm a twenty-four-year-old sitting there in a very difficult spot not knowing what to do with real conflict going on in the staff."[2]

---

2. For the 2002 Houston Texans, they had nine different offensive lineman start in a game. Only three played in all 16 games (center Steve McKinney, left tackle Chester Pitts, and right guard Fred Weary), with two of them (Pitts and Weary) being rookies. When Carr mentions signing players off the street, he may be speaking of Chad Overhauser, who was drafted in the 7th round by the Chicago Bears in 1998, but didn't play in his first game until joining the Texans four years later.

Most Quarterback Sacks, Rookie Season

Player	Team	Season	# of Sacks
David Carr	Houston Texans	2002	76
Tim Couch	Cleveland Browns	1999	56
Blake Bortles	Jacksonville Jaguars	2014	55
Jake Plummer	Arizona Cardinals	1997	52
Dieter Brock	Los Angeles Rams	1985	51
Tony Banks	St. Louis Rams	1996	48
Warren Moon	Houston Oilers	1984	47
Rick Mirer	Seattle Seahawks	1993	47
Andrew Walter	Oakland Raiders	2006	46
Jim Kelly	Buffalo Bills	1986	43
Geno Smith	New York Jets	2013	43

Most Quarterback Sacks, Season

Player	Team	Season	# of Sacks
David Carr*	Houston Texans	2002	76
Randall Cunningham^	Philadelphia Eagles	1986	72
David Carr	Houston Texans	2005	68
Jon Kitna	Detroit Lions	2006	63
Ken O'Brien^	New York Jets	1985	62
Steve Beuerlein	Carolina Panthers	2000	62
Neil Lomax	St. Louis Cardinals	1985	61
Randall Cunningham	Philadelphia Eagles	1992	60
Tony Eason^	New England Patriots	1984	59
Jeff George	Oakland Raiders	1997	58
Ryan Tannehill^	Miami Dolphins	2013	58

*Rookie Season

^Sophomore Season

Carr said he later found that the Texans offensive system he was asked to run *did* actually work. He saw a variation of it later in his career win him Super Bowl XLVI, where he was Eli Manning's backup with the New York Giants. But that was with the proper personnel, he said.

And it was also with Manning and the Giants during that time in 2008 and 2009 where Carr realized mistakes he had made while in Houston.

"When I was at Fresno State I studied film, practiced, and just went and ran it. When I got to Houston, I did the same thing; and struggled early like most young quarterbacks. I had no idea of the level I needed to get to. It wasn't until I got to New York and was around [head coach] Tom Coughlin and Eli [Manning], that's how I learned to study and prepare. I finally understood what it takes to go out there and play. It wasn't that I wouldn't stay more, stay longer in Houston. I would be there anytime as long as they asked. I would stay all day. But I didn't know what to do when I was there."

McNair said he was unaware of the Texans' staff friction then, but said he saw things the staff allowed Carr to do which bothered him. McNair said if he had it to do over again, there were things he would have never allowed.

Through nearly two decades of Texans ownership, McNair said he has learned other rookie franchise quarterback lessons. He will apply several of them with the Texans' fresh, hopeful rookie franchise quarterback Deshaun Watson.

"First, I would have a strong veteran quarterback who really set an example for the young one. We really didn't have that for David and it wasn't that he had bad habits, we just allowed things that never should have been allowed.[3] The staff used to just give him work, film, and tell him to go home and study it. He had a young child and wanted to spend time with his family. That's fine, but quarterback in the NFL is more demanding than that. His dad used to come to practice. Our practice field was down the street from the stadium. The players would walk over and back, or ride golf carts we provided or ride bikes. David would leave practice in his dad's truck. He'd come back to the locker room, get his things, and leave with his dad. The players see what is going on. We should have never allowed it. As the franchise quarterback, you need to be the first one in the building and the last one to leave more times than not.

"We never did get the offensive line right around him. We never did get the right team around him. I know that David could have been a good quarterback if we had. Great? I don't know that. But he certainly could have been in a more adequate situation."

Carr was released after the 2006 season. His team's records during his time in Houston were 4–12, 5–11, 7–9, 2–14, and 6–10.

The Carr experience left such scars on the franchise that when his younger brother, Derek Carr, also from Fresno State, was a promising quarterback prospect in the 2014 NFL Draft, the Texans would not touch him. Derek Carr, of course, is now flourishing with the Oakland Raiders.

McNair explained: "The brother is a carbon copy in many ways and the Raiders got him some help, an offensive line,

---

3. As of June 2017, the two "veteran" quarterbacks on the Texans roster are Brandon Weeden and Tom Savage, who have started a combined 27 games with a 7–20 record.

support—David never had that. I've known Derek since he was twelve years old. We loved Derek when he was coming out of college. But it would have been an adverse condition for him to come to Houston. The first time he made a mistake they would have connected him with David. It would not have been a fair chance for him. It was not a wise thing to do."

Derek Carr looks so promising now, some might question that thinking.

David Carr said he taught his brother the work ethic, the game planning, the way to be studious "like Eli Manning taught me and like Peyton Manning taught Eli and like Archie Manning taught Peyton." And David Carr, pulverized by 249 sacks as a Texan, said he learned to roll with those shots.[4]

"The sack numbers are big, they are embarrassing, and I was a big part of that," Carr said. "I should have thrown the ball away more to protect our team and myself. I should have gotten the ball out of my hands faster in certain situations. It wasn't until I got to the Giants that I learned how much defenses looked forward to playing us. They viewed us as a stat game for them. Some of that was totally my fault."

Carr says he has had several conversations with Casserly since. He said Casserly told him that if he had known the Texans could never build a line to protect him, they would not have drafted him. Carr said the lesson he learned for a rookie franchise quarterback is this: If a supporting cast is not there, "you are wasting your pick" just tossing him in.

---

4. In 94 career games played, Carr was sacked 267 times. That means he averaged being sacked 2.8 times a game!

Even though he is a Super Bowl champion, that first Texans game, that victory over Dallas, and the game that followed are the signature moments of his NFL career.

"My grandfather was there in Houston for the Dallas game, the whole family was there, and for what we hoped to be with the Houston Texans, in front of that electric crowd at home, it was a fantastic game, night, and experience. And then the next week we played at the San Diego Chargers, and [Hall of Fame linebacker] Junior Seau was in the A-gap the whole day. He nailed me seven or eight times. I stopped counting. We lost and were sort of battered. I went from the Dallas game thinking we are going to be OK to the San Diego game knowing we were in trouble. Those two games sum up my career as the Texans' quarterback. The highs and the lows and everything kind of in-between."[5]

* * *

Joey Harrington joined David Carr in the 2002 draft. Harrington went No. 3 overall to the Detroit Lions. Only four seasons later, the Lions traded Harrington to the Miami Dolphins after a combined 18–37 record in Detroit.[6]

The Detroit offense did not fit his talents, the execution surrounding him was poor, the offensive line was weak, and dysfunction was evident in the Lions' personnel approach.

---

5. The Chargers won that game, 24–3. Carr was sacked nine times on the day, with Seau having one of those as well as an interception.
6. The former No. 3 overall draft pick was traded from the Lions to the Dolphins in exchange for a sixth-round pick (No. 176 overall) in the 2007 draft.

Harrington accepts he was not good enough and did not win enough. He finished his pro career with additional seasons in Miami, Atlanta, and New Orleans. He threw 85 interceptions in 81 games.

Another pair of franchise quarterback hopefuls surfaced in the top 10 of the 2006 draft. They had met in the 2006 Rose Bowl for the National Championship, where Vince Young and Texas beat Matt Leinart and USC. In the 2006 draft, Young was the No. 3 pick by the Tennessee Titans. Leinart was taken No. 10 by the Arizona Cardinals.

Young created instant success. He was the 2006 NFL AP Offensive Rookie of the Year, and went 8–5 as a rookie starter. He also earned two Pro Bowl berths. But off-field and financial issues helped force a Titans split after five seasons. He would travel to Philadelphia, Buffalo, Green Bay, and Cleveland through 2014, before moving to the CFL in 2017. As an NFL starter, he compiled a 31–19 record. Leinart lasted fewer than five seasons in Arizona and, like Young, maturity issues surfaced. He was out of the league by 2013 with only 18 career starts under his belt (an 8–10 record).

JaMarcus Russell often competes with Ryan Leaf for the label of all-time NFL quarterback bust.

In 2007, Russell was the Oakland Raiders' and the draft's No. 1 overall pick. He was 6-foot-6, 260 pounds. He had won 21 of 24 games at LSU. He looked like a franchise quarterback who could change the NFL game. So big, with such a big arm and a capable runner, Russell was viewed as a quarterback who could do it all.

But red flags were abundant.

He arrived at the February pre-draft combine at least 15 pounds overweight. During the interview process, instead of talking about winning Super Bowls, he talked about "making a lot of money." It was Raiders head coach Lane Kiffin who stressed during the team's draft discussions that he did not believe Russell had the intangibles to make guys around him great or to lead. Whatever it is that inspires people to follow you, Russell lacked it, Kiffin insisted.

Kiffin and some Raiders scouts wanted to draft receiver Calvin Johnson.

Then Raiders owner, Al Davis, made the final call—it would be Russell.

And after a lengthy holdout, Russell was signed to a $61 million contract, with $32 million guaranteed.

"The scouting reports had said that he needed someone to make sure he got to class, that he needed someone to take him to class, and that he could be a full-time distraction," said Jon Kingdon, a Raiders personnel executive from 1978 through 2012. "But Al had made up his mind. He saw a franchise quarterback there. Then the whole contract thing set JaMarcus back and behind. Then I'm told he finally shows up, goes into his first meeting with teammates, has a song playing about 'making it rain,' and starts tossing dollar bills around. I think the players took it well. They were laughing and having fun with it. But really, that's your franchise quarterback?

"They sent him home with DVDs to watch, to study, on the offense. One time they asked him how did it go? He said it was great, he learned a lot. And the coaches happened to check the DVD, looking for something, and realized it was blank. It was an accident. But it was revealing. He just didn't do the things a quarterback must do."

Russell lasted three seasons with the Raiders, compiling a
7–18 record as a starter.[7]

Robert Griffin III posted early NFL success. Griffin, in fact,
dazzled.

In 2002, Griffin was the Washington Redskins' and the draft's
No. 2 overall pick. The Redskins invested a heavy price for him
in a trade with the St. Louis Rams to move up to that draft spot:
the Rams received three Redskins first-round picks in 2012,
2013, and 2014, and a second-round pick in 2012.

Griffin looked worth the risk. He had won the 2011 Heisman
Trophy at Baylor. During his rookie season with Washington, he
set numerous rookie passing records, even leading the team to
the playoffs. He won AP Offensive Rookie of the Year honors.

"He was a rookie, he was our future, but right away he gave
us the best chance to win," then Washington head coach Mike
Shanahan said. "He did a lot of good things."

Griffin had run a zone-read offense in college, an offense that
spreads the field and uses the quarterback's running ability as a
threat or as an actual weapon.

"Robert forced me to learn the zone read and how to coach
it," said Kyle Shanahan, then the Washington offensive coordinator and now the San Francisco 49ers head coach. "I didn't
always believe in it, but it made me a better coach.

"I'm extremely proud of what we accomplished with Robert.
He had the best rookie year for a quarterback. We put together
something suited for his talents. The NFL had a hard time trying

---

7. In 25 career starts, Russell threw over 250 yards in a game once, under
   150 yards twelve times, and never threw more than two touchdown passes.
   In addition, he threw an interception in 13 of his 25 starts.

to adjust to it. Anytime people have a lot of success, you get other people in your ear. You don't always know what you're going to get. The second year he was coming off injury. It changed things."

Griffin's knee injury late in his rookie season and surgery afterward made him want to become a pure, NFL pocket passer faster. The Redskins had told him that took time, a process that must unfold, and that the best approach was to continue running a variation of his college offense while building toward that. But Griffin wanted to move on faster. He was not interested in learning to slide to protect himself from hits. He thought the system from his rookie season would bog him down. Pigeon-hole him.

"He had no idea," Mike Shanahan said. "I think he thought he was the chosen one and that he could do anything at any time. And the owner [Dan Snyder] fostered that belief in him. I tried to tell them both that if we don't follow the adjustments to becoming a pro quarterback that he could be out of the league in two years. He had to study the game. The position. But Robert was more interested in doing it his way. He just wanted to lift weights."

Shanahan was fired after the 2013 season.

Jay Gruden replaced him and quickly butted heads with Griffin.

Only one season in, this is the way Griffin and Gruden viewed each other, both from an August 2015 training camp interview.

Griffin: "You hope it's growing. I don't know that. It's not something we talk about. People have talked about it and there is a lot out there and so many perceptions. I don't really know him and he doesn't really know me. But how could that be any other way in only one year? It takes more time than that when you are talking about any great head coach-quarterback situation, including the historical ones like Walsh-Montana and Belichick-Brady. People are complex, football is a game of complexities, and I hope we will in the future continue to move in that kind of direction."

Gruden: "You look at Robert's first year and his success—but he got hit a lot. He got hit beyond obvious injury. We don't want that for him and for any of our quarterbacks. He's just gotta make plays. The ball has to come out and go where it is supposed to go."

Griffin wound up the Redskins' third-string quarterback before he was released on March 7, 2016. He spent the 2017 season in Cleveland but was hampered by injuries before being cut after the season.

* * *

The fabrics of these stories share familiarity to Mike Martz.

Martz spent most of his NFL career working with veteran quarterbacks. His production with Kurt Warner and the Rams offered one of the NFL's most prolific offenses in a Super Bowl championship season (1999), where the Rams scored 529 points.

He worked most with veteran quarterbacks, but was exposed to rookie ones as well.

"You have the one-year wonders who light it up and the next year guys adjust to them and they do not adjust," Martz said. "You've got guys who just aren't very tough, just not competitive enough, who don't understand that the great ones don't say no—they find a way. And then you've got what is probably the worst coached position in sports. Not enough of these coaches are clear. If you have a rookie franchise quarterback, each situation is different. It's difficult to measure if he should sit or play. You've got to get a feel for the quarterback. You've got to know what's around him. It is a decision to make considering many factors."

Martz lives in San Diego. He said he received a call from representatives of both Jared Goff and Carson Wentz to work with them before the 2016 draft.

So, Martz met both quarterbacks three months before the draft on an Orange County football field.

"I didn't see anything wrong with them. They were both terrific prospects. I told them I hope and pray they go someplace where they develop quarterbacks."

In Martz's estimation, Goff did not while Wentz did.

"Jared Goff?" asked Martz. "I don't know if he can play or not, but I do know he couldn't have gone to a worse place. If you took him and switched him with Dak Prescott in Dallas, who knows what would have happened for Goff there. Goff at Cal came from an offense where they ran as many plays as they could—fast. Jared in college did an amazing job of throwing a true ball off balance, under duress, making things happen. You knew the speed of the NFL would throw that kind of timing off. But he still throws a true ball. The Rams wanted to re-wire him to what? I watched the Rams offense last season. It was awful football. There was nobody there on that staff that could teach him, develop him. You have a high-value guy like that and he went to the worst offensive place, the Rams."

The Rams 2016 season top offensive coaches were assistant head coach/offense Rob Boras and quarterbacks coach Chris Weinke.

Martz was asked if he believed new Rams head coach Sean McVay can make a difference for Goff.

"What is he, a couple of months older than Jared? They hired a buddy for Jared. The NFL has nothing to do with being the friend or the buddy of the quarterback. You've got to coach them and work them hard with respect. But buddy? And this guy is a quarterback expert? An offensive expert? Wait a minute while I puke. Right, he's going to be able to teach and handle and guide Jared through tough times because of all of his expertise and knowledge? Right. I'm not going to drink that Kool-Aid."

Martz said he does not know much about Philadelphia's offensive staff, but he does know it consists of Frank Reich, a former long-time NFL quarterback, and others with textured offensive backgrounds.

Martz is especially high on Wentz.

"Wentz ran a pro-type offense at his school and was ahead of the curve in that respect. I've never seen any young quarterback work out like Wentz did in my time with him. I saw Peyton Manning work out coming out of college. Wentz was just ridiculous, the arm strength, the overall arm. I mean, both guys are 1-2 in the draft, so, you could flip them around all day and you still have talent either way. Let's see what happens."

That is an apt refrain for all future NFL rookie franchise quarterbacks.

* * *

What makes a rookie franchise quarterback become an eventual bust? And is the title ever truly accurate and earned?

These examples illustrate that a myriad of factors affect his failure; that the simplistic description of "bust" is hardly ever completely accurate. But for some quarterbacks among this group—especially including Marinovich, Leaf, and Russell—the title sticks most. It is a pervasive and routine label when describing these three quarterbacks.

Maybe because this trio, in particular, helped create their demise with a glaring lack of attentiveness, professionalism, and maturity that cost them terribly. Their antics both on and off the field, as well as their lack of execution and focus, were as much detriments as any poor coaching or franchise planning.

Shattered dreams can occur for rookie franchise quarterbacks when they are in pitifully run franchises that stunt their development. They surely occur when the rookie sets on a bust track by not doing his part in a high-profile position for such giant stakes.

* * *

The best chance for NFL success is for the rookie quarterback and the franchise to fully embrace their roles. The quarterback must excel in all off-field responsibilities even before he attempts to elevate on the field. The franchise must provide an environment that offers clear communication and support, coupled with task-mandated coaching.

Too often, on each part, an imbalance occurs in these areas that set the entire relationship awry from the start. Too often, coaches speak in hidden messages, act in you-figure-it-out ways, and in their discipline play too many mind games. Too often rookie quarterbacks fail to execute what is required in their focus and approach to succeed. Breakdowns in communication and teaching also surface most when harsh struggles occur.

But both sides must expect storms. Both sides must embrace trials and deal with them collectively.

Even with the best intentions, the most artful plans, shattered NFL dreams are inevitable. Sometimes the player, the franchise, the connection is simply amiss. Sometimes the rookie quarterback really is a bust. Sometimes the franchise and the coaching have no clue on how to best groom him. Oftentimes, it just rolls inevitably toward disaster. Signs are missed. Relationships sour. The process wilts.

The core is rotten.

Shattered dreams result.

Chapter 6

BRAIN TRUST

One can easily find a bunch of intelligent and even brilliant quarterbacks who were not worth a nickel in the NFL.

But there has never been a franchise quarterback who did anything special for any lengthy period that did not possess football intelligence.

This is a guy who owns a DNA system that screams winner. He features a mentality that has no quit. He is one whose mental edge masters offenses and dissects defenses. He has that knack of processing information in a blink during games.

This is the way Andrew Luck was described long before he took his first live snap in the NFL.

Big-game, big-time kicker Adam Vinatieri remembers the 2012 Indianapolis Colts' first full practice, and this one rookie quarterback among them.

They had all heard of his impact at Stanford. Most of them had seen it. They hoped he could duplicate it with them. He entered as the 2012 NFL Draft's No. 1 overall pick, a new Colts glorified franchise quarterback. He arrived to replace a future Hall of Famer in Peyton Manning, who the team had drafted No. 1 overall in 1998 and had recently signed as a free agent with the Denver Broncos.

In college, Luck had excelled in intelligence, mentality, and processing skills. He had consistently flashed what experts call the natural, organic, rare "DNA" associated with the finest ever quarterbacks.

Andrew Luck just had "it."

"You come to camp and everybody pretty much knows all of the plays and some learn it a little quicker than others," Vinatieri said. "But I remember Day 1, and this guy was running the offense and executing nuances of it and changing plays at the line of scrimmage and it made you go 'Whoa!' I just remember thinking that he is not supposed to be able to do that on the first day. He's become the type of quarterback now, a lot like Peyton Manning, where he plays chess with defenses. There is something they want him to do; he forces them to play the way he wants them to. He keeps them off guard. He's really smart— beyond my comprehension."

Luck earned Pro Bowl honors in each of his first three NFL seasons. He's earned a 43–27 record in the regular season and a 2–1 record in the postseason (through the 2016 season). He has thrown 141 touchdown passes and 80 interceptions in both regular season and postseason action.

He started all 16 games as a rookie for the Colts.

"I like playing, so, of course, I loved the fact that was the approach the Colts took with me," Luck said. "I've always tried to work hard, always prepare. I think Adam is just being very nice, because I know I made my share of mistakes that first day of practice. I've always looked at every practice, every game, every season as a chance to get better."

He must. The Colts must. Because despite all of Luck's mental acumen and big plays, neither he nor the Colts have had a whiff of the Super Bowl with five full seasons under his belt.

The intelligence required to play NFL quarterback. The DNA. The mentality. The ability to process information and untangle complex defensive pass coverages.

Luck said all of those things are related and none of those traits is more important than the other. While New England Patriots head coach Bill Belichick agrees, others in the NFL disagree.

All do agree on this: Recognizing which rookie quarterbacks have it and cultivating "it" with rookie quarterbacks can be a tiresome, perplexing, wearisome task.

* * *

Intelligence is a buzzword for quarterbacks. It has been a controversial description in NFL history. Many African American quarterbacks were not awarded opportunities they deserved in the league based on ownership, coaches, and scouts determining they did not have the "intelligence" to play the position.

Though some of those walls have tumbled, NFL coaches today insist they collectively examine, grade, and place varied value on a quarterback's raw intelligence—but even more on all of the attributes including leadership, communication, toughness, and playmaking. On his winning.

More than the intelligence, they want to know how he uses his smarts to process football X's and O's.

"People read a lot into intelligence, and it can mean a lot of different things," Tony Dungy said. "There are all kinds of tests, including intelligence tests, that NFL teams use to try to measure this and other traits. But I've found that some guys are very smart who are not good at making decisions under fire. I've always focused on passing efficiency, accuracy, and decision-making. Those are the things where a rookie quarterback and all quarterbacks can really struggle."

Jon Gruden said that processing is simply recognition.

"It's communication, execution. And that processing has to be quick. It's understanding matchups. It's communicating through hand signals. It's executing a play and making it your own. It's mental quickness."

A young quarterback who talks a good mental game historically and presently grabs NFL coaches' attention. This happened for Jim Fassel when he was a quarterback at USC in 1972.

"I had the Bears, the Chargers, the Oilers, and some other teams knocking at my door before the '72 draft," Fassel said. "One of them sent a chief scout to my home. I asked him why? He said that I had scored extremely high on one of their tests. He said we always look closely at quarterbacks who score high on our tests. I was drafted by the Bears in the seventh round. I bounced around a little bit. I wouldn't say my pro career reflected the testing—a lot of good that did me."

Fassel began his coaching career with the Hawaiians of the World Football League in 1974. After several years as an assistant for several schools, he was hired as the head coach at the University of Utah, where he led from 1985 through 1989. He left college to work in the NFL as an offensive coordinator and quarterback specialist before becoming the head coach of the New York Giants from 1997 through 2003 (he led his team to Super Bowl XXXV, a loss to the Baltimore Ravens). Long regarded a quarterback guru, he did some of his best NFL work with Phil Simms, John Elway, Jeff Hostetler, and Kerry Collins.

"During my early time with the Giants, we used to give players a five-hour psychological test at the combine. Five hours! Or, we'd mail it to them and have them send it back. Sure, quarterbacks have to have average to above average intelligence, but they don't have to be Einstein. Every really good quarterback I've ever worked with has said they loved how I kept it simple. We have a lot of coaches in the NFL today who are so sophisticated, who work 24/7 game planning, being tricky and fancy. They are trying to impress. And I ask them, 'Did you ever play quarterback?' You've got two and a half seconds back there once the ball is snapped, and then you'd better do something. So, the good ones told me to make it easy for them; to understand and tell them what I wanted them to do. That works.

"I think another mistake we make with young quarterbacks is we have the offensive coordinator. *And* the quarterback coach. *And* the passing game coach. And it goes on and on. To me, that is too many people in his ear. It's just too elaborate sometimes."

Fassel ranks the "brain trust" elements of rookie quarterbacks this way:

1. Mentality
2. Intelligence
3. DNA
4. Processing

"I want to know what's really above the shoulders," Fassel continued. "What's the mentality? Where is the work ethic? Where is the leadership? Phil Simms used to pick a night with the offensive linemen, buy pizza and beer, and go over the game plan just with them. Then he'd pick another night for the receivers and running backs and do it with them. All of the really good ones are really committed. First one in, last one out. The intelligence, testing part of it is overrated. All of these traits we are talking about for rookie quarterbacks, especially as you scout them and possibly draft them, you are considering all of these things. They all have their place. It's hard to clarify. But I focus on one question when I meet with rookie quarterbacks for the first time and with players in general.

"My first question is always, 'Who is your role model?' What rings the bell is if they say their father. Or their mother. Then I ask them, 'What do your parents do?' If they say serviceman, or policeman, or something like that significant, if they say their mom is a homemaker, well, those kinds of things ring a bell, too. I give 'em an A in that area, because you know they've been brought up right. If they come up with an answer way off the cuff on their role models, that makes me nervous. Love of the game and an overriding work ethic and commitment is the road map for young quarterbacks."

Mike Shanahan agrees with Fassel that a rookie quarterback needs a strong foundation. Shanahan also said that a young quarterback cannot succeed in the NFL without intelligence and the ability to process. He thinks fearlessness is just as essential a tool to their success.

Shanahan said rookie quarterbacks in particular—and quarterbacks in general—distinguish themselves in their character, mentality, and perseverance.

"How does this quarterback handle people?" Shanahan said. "Are they a solid guy? Like the Boy Scouts ask, are they a trustworthy guy? A loyal guy? This is important. It surfaces with coaches and with teammates and even with fans. You go all the way back and talk to his high school coaches. His high school teachers. You ask them, 'How did he treat people that could do nothing for him? Does he really love the game?' Too, his attitude, especially a positive attitude, is going to affect your team. That affects the preparation. You love a guy who you can tell him something and then three weeks later he is telling you what you told him.

"And the perseverance of a guy. Can he handle all of the adversity, take all of the crap that comes with playing quarterback in the NFL? Can he handle it? Especially at the quarterback position, you have to have that."

* * *

Matt Ryan is an example of how despite a rookie franchise quarterback's commanding intelligence, he often needs time to reach the Super Bowl. He needs dynamic weapons around him to excel.

Sometimes what he thinks he knows, he doesn't. Sometimes what he figures out can be lasting.

Ryan was the Atlanta Falcons, first-round pick, No. 3 overall, in the 2008 NFL Draft. He arrived from Boston College with extremely high NFL intelligence test scores and the communication skills and arm to warrant franchise quarterback status.

From 2008 through the 2015 season he won games, threw touchdown passes, led. He was the 2008 AP Offensive Rookie of the Year. He was a Pro Bowler in 2010, 2012, 2014, and 2016.

But he lost each of his playoff games in 2008, 2010, and 2011. They call him "Matty Ice." It was meant for his cool style of play. It was growing into another meaning—the guy who freezes in the playoffs.

But the 2016 season provided his key breakthrough.

He threw for a career-high 4,944 yards. He tossed 38 touchdown passes and 7 interceptions (also a career high and low, respectively). He averaged 9.3 yards per pass when he had never managed more than 7.9, and that was in his rookie season. He won numerous awards.[1]

It took Matt Ryan his ninth NFL season to reach Super Bowl LI, but he fell short in an agonizing close overtime loss to New England. He was so close to accomplishing what he came to the Atlanta Falcons to do.

"I mean, the coaching, the players, the system, the timing, it all came together this year, as did I in growing in it all," Ryan, thirty-two, said during his 2016 season playoff run. "If you have a guy that you consider a franchise guy at quarterback, you're best off, if you believe in him, to just keep at it, keep building, give him every chance with the best you can provide to get his best. That's what happened for me."

One can tell by the way Ryan mastered all of the elements of a franchise quarterback off the field, on it, in the locker room, and in the community during the 2016 season that he is far from done. He has reached a new plateau and so have the Falcons around him; a level of confidence and production where

---

1. In 2016, Ryan was awarded the AP Offensive Player of the Year Award, Bert Bell Award (Player of the Year), AP Most Valuable Player, and PFWA MVP.

personnel and coaching changes (he lost offensive coordinator Kyle Shanahan, who became San Francisco 49ers head coach) will not derail him.

His intelligence is apparent. His DNA has long featured a stamina, a willingness to fight.

He did not adopt the mentality that, because this kind of success had not happened for him in his previous eight NFL seasons that the ninth would not be different. In 2016, he processed things faster on the field, got rid of the ball quicker, more decisively. His voice was stronger among the Falcons. Clearer. His determination was spread. He simply thought clearly and played clean.

He provided a mindset, a mental blueprint, and tactic that NFL coaches love. It is the type that they desperately seek.

One they often are bewildered in identifying while selecting rookie franchise quarterbacks.

* * *

Sean Payton knows quarterbacks. He knows offense.

The New Orleans Saints head coach has crafted a top-10 offense in every season since he arrived there in 2006. His offense has led the league in net yards five times and in scoring twice. His connection with quarterback Drew Brees is elite.

Brees had spent five seasons with the San Diego Chargers before joining the Saints with Payton in 2006.

Together they won Super Bowl XLIV.

"I would say I've coached intelligent quarterbacks who were slow processors," Payton said. "I value players processing real quickly over those players who are intelligent but slow processors. This is one of Drew Brees's strengths—processing and deciding.

I don't think that necessarily correlates to overall intelligence. It does sometimes. Quarterbacks who are extremely smart, you're trying to grade that and it is important. But some guys get the message from the coach, spit out the cadence to the players, and don't blink. Others . . . boy, it's time consuming. It is not a fatal flaw. You've just got to work at it.

"There are some physical standards. The quarterback portrait is 6-foot-2 or 6-foot-3. The weight requirement can be 210 pounds. You like a quarterback to have a strong frame, strong chassis. I look for that. Drew Brees is not that height. He's not that weight. People try to say he is an overachiever because of that. It's not true. He is a phenomenal athlete even though he is a full inch or inch and a half shorter than the prototype standard. We are talking about somebody who beat tennis pro Andy Roddick in youth tennis, that kind of athlete. When I think mentality for young quarterbacks, I think, *What's the makeup? Does he have the grit you are looking for? Is he outspoken? Confident? Arrogant? The grit?* It's attitude, it's that word grit. How are they wired?"[2]

Rookie quarterbacks need help, Payton said. In a preseason game, if the rookie quarterback is on the field with young offensive linemen and makes a mistake, it's just a mistake, he explained. But if the offensive linemen makes the mistake and the rookie quarterback is pounded, injured, or mentally scarred, it

---

2. In the past five years (2013–17), there have been twelve first-round quarterbacks drafted. Of these twelve, their average height is 6-foot-3 1/2, and their average weight is 224.66 lbs. The smallest was Johnny Manziel (6-foot, 207 lbs.), while Paxton Lynch (6-foot-7, 244 lbs.) was the largest. Aside from Manizel, no first-round quarterback drafted in the last five years has been shorter than 6-foot-2.

can be more than a mistake. It can stunt his growth. It can haunt the franchise.

Payton said NFL head coaches and offensive coaches should bear more responsibility on how rookie quarterbacks are developed.

"When you think about them processing information, it's coming in, and you wonder if they can gather it in a day or maybe two and have permanency, repeat it, and understand it," Payton said. "Can you do it next week? If you're with a quarterback and the next week is like the first day, that is not good. Some guys, all they need is one day and they've got it forever. Part of that is DNA. We're trying to have them learn, go to the board, show us in the film room, on the field, talk the topic, watch their ability to process. A better question we should be asking is how are we going to coach this player? Is he better wearing a wrist band when spitting the play out in the huddle? I don't want to eliminate the eighteen Hall of Fame quarterbacks that could be in the league just because we couldn't teach. It's fatal when we as coaches don't understand that coaching isn't always meant to be convenient. Some you can develop. We live in a world of repetition. Some might require more. Most do better on the field than in the classroom."

"Certainly, you can play that game of failure and success with rookie quarterbacks in the NFL. If the guy who failed had been somewhere else with different elements, would he have succeeded? If the guy who succeeded had been in a bad situation, would he have failed? A lot goes into your vision, and vision is critical. Without proper vision as an organization you end up minus the proper result. Periodically, a rookie comes in and he is behind an outstanding veteran. It makes a difference. He's watching him practice, how he studies film, what he had for breakfast. He's going to learn something. The young quarterback behind Drew Brees is in for a special situation."

Payton said his NFL experience has revealed that the coach-player, the teacher-student relationship must always be nurtured and that it is critical regardless of the quarterback's intelligence. He said that players' learning methods cross section in four ways—never struggles in education and football learning; never struggles in education but struggles in football learning; struggles in education but never in football; struggles in both.

He calls it good-good, good-bad, bad-good, bad-bad.

Payton is fascinated and actively in pursuit of gauging the mental side of young quarterbacks and all young players. He is certain that testing for this has its place in the NFL.

"I remember that [running back] Darren Sproles got a 9 on an educational test score when we evaluated him coming out of college, and for the test it was not a good score, not a good number. But I can't recall one time Darren Sproles when I coached him did something incorrectly. This probably exists in other sports. In baseball, when the pitcher releases the ball and before it gets to the catcher's mitt, the hitter has quick seconds to decide whether he will swing or not. An educational test is not going to tell you how proficient he will be at that. We need more data in the mental side of testing.

"You can be outstanding in algebra and history. But we are trying to understand that this guy learns this way and that guy learns that way. There are some standards. There has never been a .300 hitter in major league baseball who was lower than this number in this test, for example. How many cornerbacks who run 4.7 or worse are in our league? Maybe one? You understand and appreciate those outliers. But we've been behind, like all sports, in grading the mental. A scout will say this player can learn, it may take him some time. What does that mean? There are 50 shades of that."

Before the 2017 draft, Payton and the Saints found new resources.

"We are working with a group out of Louisville this year for the first time that has sixteen different tests in the area of processing that are trying to help us with this as we try to evolve to become better in this area of identifying. For example, there is a test given to a player where a computer screen will show 12 dots. Then three red dots are highlighted among them. The dots slowly begin to move and stop. You have to remember where they were. Then it's four red dots. Same thing. We are measuring mental traits that have developed and finalized in that way since the player was probably thirteen or fourteen years old. Running back Leonard Fournette out of this year's draft got 7 or 8 out of 12 dots. I tried it and I was done after 4. But his mind works in a way where he got 7 or 8."[3]

Consider that Fournette reportedly scored an 11 out of a possible 50 on his pre-draft Wonderlic test, an intelligence test used to gauge learning and problem solving. The test is 50 multiple choice questions to be answered in 12 minutes. The score of 20 is considered average and 10 or higher literate. A rookie quarterback's average score is reportedly 24, according to Paul Zimmerman's *The New Thinking Man's Guide to Pro Football.*

"Another test," said Payton, "is the player looks at a computer screen. He is looking at white letters. They appear—B, W, Q,

---

3. Leonard Fournette was picked No. 4 overall in the 2017 draft by the Jacksonville Jaguars.

R . . . then other letters pop up in red and blue. They move around. He has to tell you where the blue letter was. They move. They move again. He has to tell you where they moved. They get to a point where the tempo is so fast that you can't get it. You are testing focus, retention, re-focusing. You are testing attention. I'm excited about this area and we are exploring it fully. It may become a standard for learning more about all rookie players and especially rookie quarterbacks."

* * *

Payton deserves credit for identifying the intelligence, DNA, mentality, and processing ability of Drew Brees.

Some saw it at Purdue. It was there in record-setting style and production. The Chargers believed enough in it to make Brees a 2001 second-round draft pick, No. 32 overall. But that meant 31 times, that for 31 selections, he was ignored in the first round. The only quarterback chosen before him was Michael Vick, who was taken No. 1 overall by the Atlanta Falcons. But neither Vick nor any of the 31 players selected before Brees have played as long and produced as decorated a career.

Brees started slowly with the Chargers. He only played in one game as a rookie. He was 10–17 in his first 27 starts through the 2003 season, with 28 touchdowns and 31 interceptions. He began to rise in 2004, starting 15 games. The Chargers went 12–4 and Brees threw 27 touchdown passes and 7 interceptions. That same year, the Chargers drafted Philip Rivers (or rather traded for him).

And after the 2005 season, with Brees having suffered a shoulder injury and his time in San Diego ticking because of Rivers, Brees was a free agent who considered Miami and New Orleans. Miami eventually balked, concerned over his shoulder.[4]

But Payton was all in, confident the shoulder would heal and even more confident in this quarterback's intelligence, DNA, and, particularly, his in-game processing ability. In 2006, Payton was in his first season as New Orleans head coach. Payton was a former college, Arena League, and CFL quarterback. He had tutored and tailored NFL quarterbacks from 1997 through 2005 for the Eagles, Giants, and Cowboys. Payton knows quarterbacks. He saw in Brees what many in the NFL did not. He was willing to risk any concern over Brees's injured shoulder when many NFL teams were not. Because Payton knew that if the guy was healthy he could process and execute his offense in just the manner he wanted.

Payton knew that if Brees was healthy, he had his franchise quarterback in New Orleans.

Watch Drew Brees play quarterback for the Saints and it is clear how well he has mastered Payton's offense. Watch the two of them work and they are like scientists, like sculptors, carving defenses.

In 2017, Brees will enter his 17th NFL season and his 12th in New Orleans. He has led the league in passing yards seven times,

---

4. Passing on Brees, the Dolphins instead traded with the Vikings for Daunte Culpepper (in exchange for a second-round pick), who had just completed his seventh year in Minnesota but only started seven games in 2005 due to a serious knee injury. In one year with Miami, Culpepper started only four games, going 1–3.

has passed for more than 5,000 yards five times, and led the league in touchdown passes four times. He is an eventual Hall of Fame quarterback who makes decisions and gets rid of the football more quickly than any NFL quarterback. His deep-ball accuracy is uncanny.

Some of it is Payton's teaching. Most of it is Brees's DNA and ability to process information from the classroom to the practice field to the game—including his in-game adjustments.

NFL teams keep searching for the proper tools to identify these traits in rookie franchise quarterbacks.

The path, the formula to it will always include the proper mixture of coaches' and scouts' guts blended with testing/science.

Chapter 7
THE QUARTERBACK ROOM

Rookie quarterbacks longing to become franchise quarterbacks toil countless hours in the quarterback room. What and who is in that room, how he is taught, and his level of attentiveness colors his NFL foundation.

The quarterback room is the offense's engine room.

It is where I's are dotted and T's are crossed. It is the room where every offensive stone is turned. It is where quarterbacks are coached, critiqued, and groomed. It is a classroom. It is a laboratory. It is often restricted to a select group: the head coach, the offensive coordinator, the quarterback coach, and the quarterbacks.

Some NFL teams keep the room simple. They reduce it to the game plan for each week on white boards, a video screen, and a small group of desks and chairs. The desks are often oval or round in shape to induce connecting. Computer tablets are common. Other teams are more elaborate. The room is larger with more seating to accommodate rare occasions where the coaches and quarterbacks may want to meet with a particular offensive group, including wide receivers or running backs. A huge video screen centers the room. Some insert four walls of floor-to-ceiling whiteboards, encasing the room. Those whiteboards hold the entire offensive playbook, including formations, routes, verbiage, and signals for the no-huddle offense. Markers are handy to additionally scrawl and scheme, and nearly every inch of those walls is used with only three parts of the room that cannot be written on: the door, the floor, and the ceiling.

It is a clean room.

The rookie quarterback had best come with pen, pad, and computer tablet, and incessantly construct industrious notes to learn, to grow, to anchor his foundation.

"If he doesn't do that, he has no chance," said Terry Robiskie, the Tennessee Titans offensive coordinator.

Mike Martz bluntly says: "The productive guys are judicious and ask questions. That's a good quarterback room. I wouldn't tolerate if a quarterback came in there without pen and paper. A guy not paying attention, I'd fire him, I'd get rid of him that day if it was in my power."

Robiskie was a running back from 1977–81, playing with the Oakland Raiders (1977–79) and Miami Dolphins (1980–81). He has been an offensive expert with several NFL teams since 1982.

He, in fact, remembers an NFL without quarterback rooms.

"It just didn't exist when I first started coaching," Robiskie said. "The quarterbacks met in the offensive coordinator's office. Back in '82 when I was with the Raiders and we moved to LA, our offices were in an old elementary school in El Segundo [California]. We had shower curtains we would pull to help divide the spaces. When I first got to the Raiders as a player in '77, Kenny Stabler was the guy and David Humm was his backup. And their quarterback room consisted of Humm every day bringing Kenny a cup of coffee and a pack of cigarettes. That was old-time football."

Rookie quarterbacks desperately need veteran quarterbacks as mentors. And even if the backup quarterback is not a veteran, he must be a mature voice; a diligent pro who augments the rookie quarterback.

The Jets thought they had this in 2014, when they paired second-year quarterback Geno Smith with veteran Michael Vick. Smith was a hopeful franchise quarterback who in his rookie season the year before had started all 16 games. The Jets finished 8–8, and Smith won three of his final four games.

So, the 2014 season was considered a chance for the veteran Vick to guide him, teach him, be a listening ear, and counsel him on how to be a pro . . . but the Jets finished 4–12, their head coach, Rex Ryan, was fired, and the entire Jets franchise was toxic and in chaos. Smith made 13 starts, played in 14 games, and struggled despite Vick's influence. The following season produced the punch and fractured jaw from a locker room swing by teammate IK Enemkpali that knocked Smith from the starting role and out of the Jets' plans for good. He made no starts in that season and only one in 2016 before signing as a free agent with the Giants for 2017.

Before that, before the 2014 season, Vick offered a now haunting insight on his chief message to Smith before it all began. In a private interview in the Jets locker room, Vick said: "There is so much temptation out there in everything for players. There is a fine line finding the right way to think and to stay firm. It's hard to know how it will all work out for Geno. But I do know that help is going to be needed. Help in the game and everything that comes along with it. You never know what will come. It's scary sometimes. It's what we sign up for."

* * *

In the most fertile and blossoming connections, the veteran quarterback watches video in the quarterback room with the rookie and advises him before the coaches do. He is the one in the room with him on Monday mornings after an ugly loss and on Tuesdays when the rest of the team has off. He is the guy with the rookie quarterback for the first four or five minutes of halftime while coaches are making in-game adjustments; in that halftime locker room setting, the veteran and rookie form their own consulting version of a mini quarterback room. He does the same on the sidelines during games. He is the pro who shows the rookie how to become one.

In the thirty-five years that Robiskie has been a coach, he has seen several instances of this special combination. He saw it between Gary Kubiak and John Elway in Denver. Between both Chris Redman and Matt Schaub for Matt Ryan in Atlanta. Between Frank Reich and Jim Kelly in Buffalo. Between Kelly Holcombe and Peyton Manning in Indianapolis.

One in today's game that Robiskie finds particularly singular takes place in Carolina.

Derek Anderson will enter his 14th NFL season in 2017. He has played for three NFL teams, played in 73 NFL games, and was a Pro Bowl quarterback in 2007 for the Cleveland Browns.[1] He joined the Panthers in 2011—the same year that they drafted rookie franchise quarterback Cam Newton with the No. 1 overall pick. Newton enters his seventh NFL season in 2017. Anderson is thirty-three, Newton is twenty-seven. Anderson has been with

---

1. That was also the last season in which the Browns had a winning record.

Newton since Newton's first day in the league. Newton considers him a respected voice of trust and teaching.

"Seven years in the NFL is a long time for a backup quarterback and a starting quarterback to work together," Robiskie says of Anderson and Newton. "Anderson was a decent quarterback. He had some success. But he's like Tylenol for Cam. He makes a lot of Cam's headaches go away. We don't know if Derek Anderson is too old now to play. But what we do know is he is indispensable to Cam. You watch Cam score and the first person he goes to on the sideline to seek is not the offensive coordinator, not other teammates—he's looking for Derek Anderson."

That is because Derek Anderson is constantly looking out for Cam Newton.

For the rookie quarterback, this connection can be prickly. The New York Giants selected Cal quarterback Davis Webb in the third round of the 2017 draft. The Giants hope that Webb can develop into a franchise quarterback. The goal is that one day he can replace current starter Eli Manning, who was drafted in 2004 as the No. 1 overall pick, won two Super Bowls, and enters his 14th NFL season in 2017.

How much does a veteran quarterback embrace tutoring a rookie quarterback who wants his job? Manning likely will be classy about it. But Manning surely clicks with the track and view that Philip Rivers took with the Los Angeles Chargers on their 2017 draft. Before it, Rivers, who like Manning was drafted in 2004, said he understood that the Chargers need to plan for the future. But Rivers said if they drafted a quarterback, they could plan on that guy "sitting for a while." Rivers had no intention of his play declining or losing his job anytime soon. Once the draft was over and the Chargers had not drafted a quarterback in the seven rounds offered, Rivers said "it was probably a good idea" that the Chargers didn't do so.

"Yeah, I don't know if it would have been real good," Rivers said. "Not that I would ever shy away from anything, but that would have been an indication to me that we're looking down the road. We're not really sure we can win right now, so we're gonna go ahead and take a quarterback at seven and we'll let you hang on as long as you can, then we're gonna move on. You know what I mean?"

Eli Manning knows exactly what he means, even though the Giants used their 2017 first-round pick to support him with another offensive weapon: sleek Ole Miss tight end Evan Engram. Manning is astute enough to remember the role in 2004 that Hall of Fame quarterback Kurt Warner played for him as a veteran mentor and guide. How that will translate in his relationship with Webb is unknown. Manning filled the role nicely with David Carr. He says he will do it again with Webb.

"I told him to stop calling me sir," Manning, age thirty-six, said of Webb, age twenty-two. "I understand they have to draft a quarterback among other players who are going to help down the road." Clearly, Manning sees Webb as a "down the road" thing. But he also realizes that "tomorrow's" quarterback can in this shock and awe league become "today's" starter.

Giants head coach Ben McAdoo attempted to take some sting away for Manning on the Webb selection by declaring that it was not Manning's job to coach or develop Webb; that it was Manning's job to prepare and play his best football.

Surely McAdoo and all of the Giants know that the best thing for Webb's growth is an open and inviting Eli Manning who willingly helps to teach the rookie on how to become a pro. This setup can help vault a rookie quarterback or be an obstacle he must overcome. It takes a strong, talented, tough rookie to rise beyond a faulty quarterback room.

"You have to have chemistry in that quarterback room, because the way a rookie quarterback develops and the relationships he builds is huge," Tony Dungy said. "They're in that quarterback room at least three times a day. There is a lot of information flowing in that room. It could have been a real headache in Dallas if Tony Romo had taken a different approach with Dak Prescott. I think everyone knows that when Aaron Rodgers (in 2005) joined the quarterback room with Brett Favre in Green Bay, that was an awkward room. I don't know how much mentoring and support was going on in there. From what I understand, not much."

* * *

Every day is a learning process in the quarterback room.

The rookie quarterback starts with an installment process of the offense where the basics are covered, from the huddle to barking the play to taking the snap. The details are mesmerizing, tantalizing. He is learning checkoffs, checkdowns, the running game, defensive strategies, you name it.

"From the start, if he doesn't come each day into that quarterback room having studied the night before everything he learned and did the day before, he has no chance to keep up," Mike Shanahan said. "He's got too much to do, too much to learn to do it any other way. He has to have the self-discipline to not only understand the big picture, but want to learn the big picture."

As Doug Williams said, the room flows if everyone in it knows their role.

"I think of it as school, as a classroom. The quarterback room is where you talk about what you like in an offense, what you don't like, the what ifs. The teacher, the coach, is up front and the pupils, the quarterbacks, are in the back. What happens in that room sets the tone for what happens in practices and in games."

Having the wrong connection between the head coach and his offensive staff—especially the offensive coordinator—can lead to ruination for a rookie quarterback, says Tampa Bay coach Dirk Koetter. We saw this with the New York Jets in 2014 when the team sank to a 4–12 record and head coach Rex Ryan and offensive coordinator Marty Mornhinweg dueled over a preferred run-first offense (Ryan's preference), opposed to a pass-first offense (Mornhinweg's preference).

The two coaches nearly came to blows over their disagreements in a staff meeting and had to be separated by other coaches. Both were fired after the 2014 season and not only did the development of Geno Smith suffer but the entire team sank.

This happens throughout NFL history; NFL head coaches who want their offensive and defensive coordinators to coach freely, to coach with imagination, only to find it difficult to reel them in when the head coach chooses or when warranted. NFL head coaches have become more careful in this setting, understanding that by allowing massive, runaway control to their coordinators can lead to the team losing its head coach's voice and imprint. NFL head coaches nowadays more frequently tell their coordinators up front how it will be—that their coordinators are in charge until they aren't.

Dirk Koetter said it had better be this way, as that is part of the foundation for Buccaneers franchise quarterback Jameis Winston's early success.

"You get fired when you are not in perfect step with the offensive coordinator and in your plan for the rookie franchise quarterback. I mean, you just have to be thinking alike when that is the guy in the quarterback room with the quarterback. It's all about being in sync."

* * *

As a head coach, Mike Martz was also his own offensive coordinator.

He said that a typical work week began with game planning on Mondays and Tuesdays. On Wednesday mornings at 7 a.m., he would meet with his quarterbacks in the quarterback room to go over the game plan. The team meeting followed at 9 a.m. Players then broke into position meetings and the quarterbacks returned to their room to hear the game plan for a second time for an additional two hours. The quarterbacks then met with their quarterback coach to review film. A half-hour, walk-through install followed. Then lunch. Then the quarterbacks met again before practice. Then practice. Then review of the practice tape with the quarterbacks.

Martz worked with veteran quarterbacks Kurt Warner, Marc Bulger, and Trent Green for most of his career. So, a play like TWINS RIGHT, SCAT RIGHT, 525, F-POST, SWING was nomenclature easily identified by his quarterbacks.

Not so easily for rookie quarterbacks.

"The biggest aspect of all is detail," Martz said. "These guys must study and retain and pay attention to detail to have success. Learning how to prepare in the NFL is the big thing for rookie quarterbacks. There is so much to know—the protections, the run game. You're trying to prepare the quarterback for all of the things he will see. The quarterback might ask 'What do I do when I see this coverage?' If you don't have an answer, you are not doing your job.

"It's a game of reaction. You don't have time to think too much. You are meeting with the quarterbacks three or four times a day. A lot is going on in that room. It's a secured room. You don't want too many people in there. The players will separately get the parts of the game plan that pertain to them. That quarterback room has to be confidential and all about personnel. Guys must speak freely. It builds a bond. You are constantly talking, writing. I am doing most of the talking in the quarterback room. It is a lot of teaching. You don't have a lot of two-way talking going on. You just don't have time. It's like going to college. You're getting great information. I'm hard on them initially. I'll ask them, 'What do you mean you don't know? We just covered this!' I've found that second-day and beyond drafted quarterbacks sometimes really struggle in this area."

Doug Williams disagrees with Martz on the frequency of back-and-forth communication between the offensive coordinator and quarterbacks. Williams believes it should be the staple of the room, that there is no such idea as too much give-and-take.

Los Angeles Rams head coach Anthony Lynn agrees with Williams.

"I want that quarterback room to be really interactive. I don't want the coach talking all of the time. I want the quarterback to feel like it is his offense. I want him to speak up. I want it to be like a partnership. I want the quarterback to be a big part of the install. I want that quarterback to be like a coach."

Chris Simms has seen nearly every angle of the quarterback room.

He played at the University of Texas before being drafted by Tampa Bay in the third round in 2003. He played in Tampa Bay from 2003–07; in Tennessee in 2008; in Denver in 2009; and finally back to Tennessee in 2010 before retiring.

Each step of his career, his quarterback room experience shifted.

"In 2003, in my first year in Tampa, Shaun King and Brad Johnson were in the quarterback room and early on Jim Miller was in there, too," Simms said. "It was a good group. They made the room comfortable. They let you speak freely. Shaun was closer to my age and he had young energy and had some early NFL success. Brad was the wily veteran who had just come off winning the Super Bowl. Brad gave me tidbits of advice and was just great on a daily basis. He helped me with thought processes that went along with a play. If I made a good play in training camp or practice, he let me know. That can be rare. Sometimes, it's just not like that. Some guys want to compete so hard that they don't want to give you credit in front of the coaches.

"As a rookie, you are so green, everything is so new, the forces in your life. The draft is over and you get to your new team and dive into the playbook. You try to figure out where you will live. I had a room with Jim Miller. I'd come in at night and he was there, into his playbook, studying. I was like, 'Damn, he's been in the league a long time and he's really getting into that playbook. I think I'd better do that, too.'"

Jon Gruden was the head coach and Stan Parrish was the quarterback coach.

"Gruden used to walk into the quarterback room saying he wanted guys that love football," Simms said. "He had great energy. That helps make a great quarterback room, too."

By the 2005 season, Simms was the Tampa Bay starter. He found that Wednesdays were his signature biggest day of the work week. He would arrive at the team facility at 6:30 a.m. He first studied film. First- and second-down offense would be featured at practice on those days, so Simms focused on that and on some of the film he had watched the night before when he was handed a semi-game plan. From 7:30 a.m. until 8:30 a.m., the quarterbacks gathered in the quarterback room.

"It was nothing special," Simms said. "A big screen in the front, a huge whiteboard on each side, six chairs, and a desk with a chair behind it for Gruden to sit and flip the screen and go to work."

The team meeting was at 8:45 a.m. The offensive game plan was dissected from 9 a.m. until 11 a.m. A walkthrough at 11:20 a.m. Lunch at 12:15 p.m. Back in the quarterback room from 12:30 p.m. until 1:15 p.m. to review film designed for practice. Practice afterward until 3:45 p.m. Back to the quarterback room to watch film of that day's practice. Discuss Thursday's practice, too, which would focus on third-down offense. From 6:30 p.m. to 7 p.m. review more third-down tape. Leave the facility near 7:30 p.m.

"And the next morning," said Simms, "show up and do it all over again."

When Simms arrived in Tennessee in 2008, his quarterback room included Vince Young and Kerry Collins.

"It was a total role reversal now. Kerry was established. I wasn't 100 percent healthy yet from my spleen injury. [Coach] Jeff Fisher had also brought me in there to help Vince. I knew Vince from Texas, he was a freshman when I was a senior. I was now the veteran mentor. It was a different vibe from Jon Gruden. With Gruden, the quarterback room was an event. With [Titans offensive coordinator] Mike Heimerdinger it was like, 'This is the game plan, this is how I teach it, this is what I expect to get done.' Not the showmanship of Gruden. Not a lot of fancy story telling. He was real matter of fact.

"Kerry was quiet, but I could approach him and ask questions. Vince and I were more social with the team. Vince had a lot of things on his plate. He didn't grow up with the greatest upbringing ever seen. I found myself trying to be the angel on his shoulder and help him out. There is a lot of crap that comes with being an NFL quarterback, a lot to sort out and get over and around. And that is especially the case for a rookie franchise quarterback. It was Vince's third year when I got there, but he had already seen a lot, done a lot, and been through a lot."

The next year when Simms arrived in Denver, coach Josh McDaniels and quarterback Jay Cutler had just resolved their nasty split—with Cutler being traded to Chicago. Simms found Kyle Orton and rookie Tom Brandstater in the quarterback room. Mike McCoy was the quarterback coach.

But McDaniels was more like Gruden, often leading the quarterbacks in the quarterback room.

"Kyle and I were similar age and had similar NFL experience. Tom was the rookie. We treated him like our family dog. We made fun of him. We made him go get the paper. Oh, definitely yeah, that happened to me as a rookie in Tampa. I was the quarterbacks' family dog and the entire team's family dog. Shaun King made sure I brought him food for the plane rides. I had to take luggage to guys' rooms on road trips. I had to have a can of

Skoal 24/7 for Warren Sapp. I was Warren Sapp's do-it guy. But I know Tom was a part of a great room in Denver. And when I think about that rookie experience for me, it brings a big smile to my face."

His final NFL quarterback room was in a return to Tennessee in 2010. Kerry Collins and rookie Rusty Smith were in it. Vince Young was in and out of it, nursing an injury.

"It was a weird room. I was bitter. I had a good training camp and preseason and they released me to keep Rusty Smith. They brought me back midseason and I was still angry about it. But Rusty was very respectful. Just the way it was constructed and the way I was in and out and the way Vince was in and out, it was weird. The rookie quarterback drafted highly walks into that quarterback room and can feel the wrath of the veteran starter. It can be a bad mix if the veteran guy is not accepting. It shouldn't be a personal competition in there. You don't worry about rooting against your teammate. You don't want him to fail on play No. 20 in practice. You just bring and show what you have. You let it be known, 'I've got something for you.' But there are times that the rookie quarterback gets treated like an insignificant punk in the quarterback room."

* * *

It was a wide open quarterback room for the Buffalo Bills in the 1990s, just like their high-wire, frenetic, explosive no-huddle offense that led them to four consecutive Super Bowl appearances.

Jim Kelly was the team's starting, dynamic franchise quarterback. He played two seasons for the Houston Gamblers in the old United States Football League (USFL) before joining the

Bills in 1986. Eleven seasons later and he had passed for 237 touchdowns en route to his Bills jersey (No. 12) being retired in 2001, and a year later reaching the Pro Football Hall of Fame in Canton.

"For me, it was a pretty cool quarterback room," Kelly said. "I had Ted Marchibroda as the offensive coordinator and Jim Shofner as the quarterback coach for most of the time in Buffalo. [Backup quarterback] Frank Reich and myself, we'd get in there with the coaches and it was wide open thinking. Frank and I had drawn up some plays on our own and we had a lot of input. We'd share that in the quarterback room. I called the plays for the last six years of my NFL career. The biggest thing coming out of that quarterback room is that the offense had to respect you. The entire team had to respect you.

"We broke down film in there. We learned how to watch film. We looked at corners and defensive backs. We learned how to pinpoint when the defense was blitzing and when it was zone or man coverage. If the corners looked at you a lot before the snap, there was probably pressure coming and they had some kind of help. If they hardly looked at you, they were probably in man coverage across the field, completely focused on their coverage in that situation. It's things like that that come out of that quarterback room."

Kelly insists all rookie quarterbacks must have a veteran next to them, and that the rookie must listen. He said the most important thing a rookie quarterback can learn on the way to becoming a franchise quarterback is that it's not as important *what* he says as much as *how* he says it to those around him.

"He has to be all ears and he has to take great notes. And, maybe not right away but, he can't wait too long for this, he has to ask questions. Don't hesitate with that. If he is on his own away from the building and thinks of a question, write it down to ask for later—when you come back to the quarterback room. Young quarterbacks can be too hesitant. If you don't know, ask! Sure, he wants to feel like he belongs. And maybe he doesn't want to be embarrassed by asking in front of others. But, I tell you this: The worst thing a rookie quarterback can do is try to learn only by his mistakes on the football field. That's the worst thing. You learn by asking questions before you make that mistake on the field and by asking questions after you make that mistake. That's my message to them—don't be afraid."

* * *

From the time the rookie franchise quarterback is drafted in April until he reaches his regular season end in January with a hopeful eye toward the playoffs, it is in the quarterback room where he is mentally and emotionally sharpened. What and who is in that room, how he is taught, and his level of attentiveness inside it colors his NFL foundation.

Robiskie said it is not uncommon in the NFL that the only people who enter the quarterback room are the owner, the head coach, the offensive coordinator, the quarterbacks—and the custodian. No lock is required, he said. Everybody knows. Everybody follows. Robiskie, despite being the offensive coordinator and the principal voice of the Tennessee offense, said he has so much respect for the room and the process created in it that when the quarterback coach and quarterbacks are inside, he knocks on the door and asks permission before entering.

"The rookie quarterback, he's got to learn how to earn, demand, command the players' love, respect, and leadership," Robiskie said. "He has to learn that when he walks out of that quarterback room and into the locker room that everybody in that room looks up to him, respects him, and sees him as a leader. He does not have to walk in there yelling and screaming and cussing. Not that. Just walk in and there is something about him that demands respect that he's earned. Swagger walking through the door. Swagger when he steps into the huddle. It's there before a word comes out of his mouth. This is the equivalent of what you want from this guy—for him to be able to tell his teammates in the huddle, 'This is what we're going to do. We're going to walk to New York, go to the middle of the Brooklyn Bridge, and jump our asses off.' And the huddle should say, 'Let's go!'"

* * *

Veteran quarterbacks, especially successful ones, often take control of their quarterback room. They ask the backups to research and find anwers to specific questions. They use their backups like an extra coach, asking their thoughts on decisions already made about how to handle a blitz pickup or deep linebacker drop. They use them as an additional pair of eyes and ears.

But the rookie quarterback in that room enters wide-eyed and all ears. The quicker he picks things up, the more gets tossed his way. The more he acts like a pro, the more he is treated like one.

Deshaun Watson, as he steps into the mix with the Houston Texans, said he understands this. He expects his quarterback room experience in Houston to be essential.

"You hear the term listening and learning like a sponge and I think that is exactly what I will do," Watson said. "I think you walk in there knowing what you did in college only gets you through the door. I had good preparation in film study at Clemson. We knew what we were doing with our offense and what defenses were doing to us. I know football is football, but I also respect the fact that the NFL game is bigger and larger and even more demanding. I'm not going to miss a thing in that room."

The Texans say that the reason they drafted Watson and invested so much in trade value to move up in the draft for him is that he won at Clemson. Almost that simple. He won big games in big moments. He played big.

The Texans have won games in recent seasons, but have not won big. They want Watson to be the franchise quarterback to win them a Super Bowl. To win a few, actually.

And they are certain that part of the reason he has won so consistently at every previous level of football is his willingess to get in the quarterback room, translate it to the practice field, and translate that into winning play in games.

Brandon Weeden, thiry-three, has played for Cleveland, Dallas, and Houston in his five NFL seasons. He was the veteran quarterback on the Texans roster when Watson was drafted. Tom Savage was considered the starter.

Watson's vault to the starting role will be impacted by his work in the quarterback room and by those in it. That is the case for all rookie franchise quarterbacks.

It is a prime vehicle for learning to speak the NFL quarterbacking language, and where foundations are built that last.

Chapter 8

THE FUTURE

On the night of April 27, 2017, a night that was not too hot, not too cold, but just right, more than 100,000 frisky football fans caroused around the Philadelphia Museum of Art. They expected compelling action in the 2017 NFL Draft. It surfaced in a spectacle, a sprint, a launch for rookie franchise quarterbacks.

Three teams—the Chicago Bears, Kansas City Chiefs, and Houston Texans—executed brave, brash, risky trades to leap higher in the first round and snatch quarterbacks. Chicago elbowed from No. 3 to No. 2 for North Carolina's Mitchell Trubisky. Kansas City jolted from No. 27 to No. 10 for Texas Tech's Patrick Mahomes. Houston prodded from No. 25 to No. 12 for Clemson's Deshaun Watson.

It is the latest example of where the NFL lives and where it is heading in the hunt for rookie franchise quarterbacks.

Jump into the draft's top tier, or hit the latter rounds and hope. Maybe pick one early and pick one late in the same draft. Select one every year in the draft if you must. Trade for one already on another team, though few let such value go.

Just keep swinging—until you connect.

And if you do, if he exhibits the elusive fabric of a franchise quarterback, do you start him instantly or sit him? Do his leadership and communication skills soar? Is the relationship between the quarterback and head coach in sync? When the gamble clicks, why? If he becomes a bust, why? How is his intelligence, DNA, and processing ability aptly identified? What role does the quarterback room play in his development?

"I mean, if you could pick those things out and make it clear what the answers are, you could make a lot of money because those are things that everybody is still looking for, still looking to answer," Los Angeles Chargers offensive coordinator Ken Wisenhunt said.

So, they just keep swinging.

"I think the significance of the position has gradually increased over the years," Sean Payton said. "Make no mistake about it, twenty-five years ago it was important to have a good signal caller, a guy who touched the ball on every play. But now teams' philosophy and approach is we have to have someone at that position to help us be successful over a period of time. History has taught us that."

No agent has represented more No. 1 draft picks (eight) than Leigh Steinberg, who has also represented more than 60 first-round picks. His first quarterback was Steve Bartkowski, selected No. 1 by Atlanta in 1975. His latest is Mahomes from the 2017 draft.

The rookie quarterback who is drafted highly is described by Steinberg as a rock star—a recipient of enormous attention bordering on idol worship. So, Steinberg demands that his quarterbacks establish roots in their new communities with foundations and charities—he thinks it increases their honor and humility. He constantly reminds his quarterbacks that they are under an intense microscope and are always at maximum risk, especially via today's social media.

He describes the complex NFL system for rookie quarterbacks and the "dearth" of proper NFL coaching for young quarterbacks as a reason why many of them suffer through "disturbed, kiltered" development.

"The so-called franchise quarterback is so under fire," Steinberg said. "You are always trying to help them get to a place where they can play with a quiet mind. It is the franchise's responsibility and mine as his representation to spin down expectations, especially for the rookie quarterback who starts right away. Public pressure escalates it and we have to spin it down effectively with constant and effective messaging. And this is what all quarterbacks, but especially the rookie quarterback who is a starter, needs: a safe haven. The nature of his job is highly strung. They need a person, a place where they can go and be open and hurt and honest and it will be accepted. Somewhere they can go when the cold side of pro football has gotten to them and they can release and it not be held against them. Somebody in the organization has to be that for them.

"We are grinding up these quarterbacks at a high rate of attrition and teams keep reaching for more of them. It is an imperfect, dilapidated, flawed process how these quarterbacks are developed and there is 24/7, micro-media coverage of that process. Teams have to get a better grip on the process—we all do—or it will just be round and round you go."

There is not a uniform approach. That is part of the allure of the NFL, where 32 teams have 32 different views on what does and does not work. On what blueprint they will create and follow. And that is complicated further by their penchant to change blueprints, sometimes smack in the middle of their processes.

"Developing quarterbacks is different, but still under the same umbrella as developing all young players," Bill Belichick said. "In the end, every team/coach has to figure out the best way to develop these players individually and as a group. For us, it changes every year with every player and we are constantly trying to evaluate the best way to make it all work and fit together. Again, player development extends well beyond the players' rookie year. Sometimes there is little visible progress in the first year and the changes are not evident until the next or later years."

* * *

Every quarterback is different. It can be likened to a parent with more than one child—a parent knows that each one learns in different ways. Most quarterbacks are elite athletes. Their competiveness and pride are often extreme.

They cannot be force-fed. Some are ready as rookies, while others need time to develop. Who are the players around him? Are his coaches adjusting to his strengths? Is the rookie quarterback investing proper time and effort? Does he understand that he must dominate the game mentally? Is the coach seeing the game through the quarterback's eyes and vice versa?

The NFL has learned that what you see early is not always an indication of what they become, whether that is from awful to elite or elite to awful. Consider the fast starts of Rick Mirer and Robert Griffin III and how they fizzled. Consider the woeful beginnings of Troy Aikman and Drew Brees and their Hall of Fame–laced careers that followed.

Twenty-six quarterbacks are in the Hall of Fame from the NFL's modern era. Of those, twelve were first-round picks. Three were No. 1 overall (Terry Bradshaw, John Elway, and Troy Aikman).[1]

Of those twenty-six quarterbacks, only two started all 16 games of their rookie seasons (Warren Moon and Jim Kelly). Three didn't start any games their rookie season (Brett Favre, Ken Stabler, and Kurt Warner). Five started one game (Len Dawson, Bobby Layne, Joe Montana, Bart Starr, and Roger Staubach).

But the NFL's new landscape is to consistently play them now, play them faster. Start him in an instant if you can. Or sit him at the start but get in him in at least mid-season or beyond. Push it, tweak it, see what he can handle. Find out if he is indeed a franchise quarterback so, if not, you can immediately start the quest, the gamble once again.

All of these essential ingredients and factors make finding and properly employing and grooming rookie franchise quarterbacks a potentially tortuous, convoluted exercise.

* * *

What do you do with a rookie quarterback smack in the middle of a lockout offseason due to collective bargaining disputes between owners and players?

This was an atypical scenario for the Cincinnati Bengals in the 2011 season. How the Bengals handled it serves as a model for

---

1. Joe Namath in 1965 was selected No. 1 overall in the AFL draft, but No. 12 in the NFL draft. Steve Young signed with the USFL out of college, and was drafted No. 1 overall in the 1984 NFL Supplemental Draft.

future teams drafting franchise quarterbacks under this circumstance and for grooming franchise quarterbacks in general.

The lockout lasted from March 12 through July 25. The lone league and team major working business that was allowed during that time was the April 28–30 NFL Draft.

The Bengals selected quarterback Andy Dalton in the second round, pick No. 35 overall. Jay Gruden, now the Washington Redskins head coach, was the Bengals offensive coordinator, his first season in that role with the team.

"There were four or five quarterbacks taken before Andy, but he was ready," Gruden said. "He had a lot of starts at TCU. He came from an NFL-styled offense. He had great work ethic and study habits. And he was a rookie quarterback immediately named the starter by us who had little competition. He got all of the reps in training camp and moving on. That helps. When a rookie is competing with a veteran, he stands on the sidelines a lot and then all of a sudden it can be, 'You're in now!' That's tough on them. Repetition is king for quarterbacks."

Whether it was calling the plays in the huddle or pre-snap reads or audibles or managing red zone situations, short yardage, or third down, Dalton displayed an instant knack for it all. He won nine games as a rookie and helped boost the Bengals into the playoffs.

Dalton focused on reacting and playing. Football is a game of reaction. The media expected the Bengals to stink in 2011.[2] That set a cool climate. Dalton said the team focused on proving

---

2. From 1968–2010, the Bengals had made the playoffs nine times. In Dalton's six seasons with the team, they have made the playoffs five times (only missing the playoffs in 2016).

them all wrong. He said gaining instant experience was the best learning tool.

"The thing that was different about my rookie year was it was a lockout year, too," Dalton said. "I had none of the offseason program. But the thing that was nice about it was it was a new offense for everyone. It was Jay's first year and it wasn't me playing catch-up—we all learned the offense on the fly together. It was quick throws and then shots down the field, and that's what we did at TCU. I think it was one of the reasons they wanted me here. It was not like I was doing something I had never done before. By the time the collective bargaining agreement was complete and the lockout was over, I reported with the team the last week of July. Training camp started a couple of weeks later. Two weeks after that was the first preseason game."

Dalton became the first quarterback in league history not drafted in the first round to start all 16 regular season games.[3] He became the first rookie quarterback in league history to pass for more than 3,000 yards and throw at least 20 touchdown passes while leading his team to a winning record. Since then, four quarterbacks have joined him in that illustrious group: Robert Griffin III, Andrew Luck, Russell Wilson, and Dak Prescott. In his 31–10 playoff loss against Houston rookie starter T. J. Yates, the pair became the first rookie quarterbacks in league history to start in the same playoff game.

Dalton said the 2011 Bengals offense was tailored to his strengths—the quick throws, the movement. The Bengals defense

---

3. Since Dalton, there have been four quarterbacks who have accomplished the same feat: Russell Wilson (2012, SEA, 3-75), Geno Smith (2013, NYJ, 2-39), Derek Carr (2014, OAK, 2-36), and Dak Prescott (2016, DAL, 4-135).

was capable. The run game featured Cedric Benson, a consistent 1,000-yard rusher.

Dalton's Bengals draft class also included vibrant receiver A. J. Green. That was significant.

"When you come in with a great receiver like that, you both work from the ground up, you build a chemistry that should last," Dalton said. "I feel like I picked things up quickly. I spent a lot of time learning how to change the play based on the defense and how to put our offense into a good play. As a rookie quarterback, the last thing you want to do is have your knowledge of the offense continually questioned. You just have to know it and that way you spend more time figuring out the defense. Rookie quarterbacks come to learn that NFL defenses are way more complicated than college ones. People talk about the speed of the game. But it's not the skill positions outside—everybody in college, like the pros, has fast people out there. It is the difference in the speed up front. You've got to get the ball out a lot faster than in college.

"Rookie quarterbacks of the future need the offense tailored more to what they are good at. You may be running a different offense than he had in college but, at the end of the day, for the rookie quarterback to be successful, if he is good at something, do that. It really helps. The spread offenses in college don't give them a lot of reps on timing routes. The rookie must learn to throw when the receiver is not open yet. You have to throw them open more on this level. You have to make sure you get your footwork down and match it up with certain routes."

Dalton handled adversity as a rookie throughout his lofty games and his lousy ones, through the big moments and the tough ones. Jay Gruden said that is the "No. 1 trait for a talented rookie quarterback in what he called 'the toughest position in sports, bar none.'"

Jay Gruden said that sure, physical toughness matters. But mentally handling success and failure, diverse teammates, receivers who want the ball, running backs who want the ball, offensive linemen who may be peeved that the rookie ruined their blocking scheme by panicking and scrambling into trouble, the coach yelling in his ear, the fans on top of him, Twitter lighting him on fire . . .

"It's tough," Gruden said. "But the game is going in a direction for rookie quarterbacks where we are seeing a lot of run-alter type of passes, quick passes to build his confidence and rhythm. Quick throws, bubble screens, even jet sweeps. They not only keep defenses off balance but give the quarterback a chance to find his rhythm. It's simple throws that let the receiver do the work for you. It's becoming a big factor for these young quarterbacks."

* * *

Rookie quarterbacks must appreciate detail. They must study and retain and pay attention to detail to have success. They must learn how to prepare.

Sometimes they enter the NFL lacking in those skills.

"College football now has gone in another direction," Mike Martz said. "They just run as many plays as they can and they don't teach them anything. Most of these young college quarterbacks can't go to a board and fully describe a play in great detail."

But it is not due to a lack of talent, says Chris Simms.

He focuses on the coaching on both the college and pro levels.

"More than ever, there is a lack of good quarterback coaches and offensive coordinators, and for some reason we keep recycling the old and bad ones," Simms said. "It's like a fraternity sometimes in the NFL—'I've been around since 1942 . . .' so, sure, let's give him another job. The coaching is huge. It's huge to a rookie quarterback's success when they don't fit the offense around what he does well. The spread offense they are running in college is not going to be run in the NFL. The fullback was used a ton, two tight ends a ton, by New England and Atlanta and they just made the last Super Bowl. There is more of a learning process for the rookies. You have to keep it simple. Expand off the things the quarterback does well."

Simms says that sometimes the spread offense is used as an excuse for some and as a criticism for others. He believes Jared Goff received more praise coming from it than Patrick Mahomes or Deshaun Watson did. Simms is not alone in thinking that some racial factors are still at play in assessing college quarterbacks.

Simms insists that though Vince Young in 2006 was drafted before Matt Leinart, that neither Leinart in that draft nor Tim Tebow in the 2010 draft should have been high picks. Leinart went at No. 10 and Tebow at No. 25.

"I saw Matt Leinart and Tim Tebow in college throw 3-yard passes to guys like Reggie Bush and others who ran 90 yards with it," Simms said. "And people go, 'Wow!' And both quarterbacks get drafted very high. You have to evaluate the players a little better than that. We have to continue to look for new ways to re-invent the evaluation process, because it gets off track from basic things and that leads to more busts."

Dick Vermeil says that NFL coaches need to vary their coaching more. For example, run their chosen practice plays in the red zone not all at once, rather at different intervals in practice. He advises them to create more sudden situations in practices for rookie quarterbacks that are more similar to what happens in games.

This is an approach that centers on coaching in a "situational football" style that Bill Belichick and others have long emphasized and employed.

But there is nothing that can displace the value of a coach's pure, competent teaching skills.

"How do they watch film?" Sean Payton asks. "Not just some games. But it has to be more in situations. What does the defense do when you play three wide receivers? And beyond that, what does it do on first down and on third down when you play three wide receivers? That is the art of teaching. We can generalize teaching the game, but what happens if we teach in a specific way for quarterbacks? Repeat and go over subjects again before going onto the next subject. You know, we're not getting paid by the word. Sometimes too much can be too confusing."

College coaches can be sensitive. NFL coaches can be sensitive. They both attempt to brush off criticisms that often are brutally dispensed toward them from every angle.

"But the better ones start to think outside of the box," Anthony Lynn said. "They embrace the use of tools like virtual reality. It's a tool that just gives the quarterback another look. It can increase focus. It's no different from a dream. A mental exercise. If we are going to throw these rookie quarterbacks into the fire, we can't give them enough things like this to help them speed up the process. Be more innovative. Watch it with the install. I've seen initial install of plays since I was a young coach up until now go from 16 plays to 17 to 32 to 33 to 59. Slow down with that. Let's get them good at something. Create some confidence and more self-awareness and build from that."

As noted earlier, this is the approach that Kyle Shanahan initially took with Robert Griffin III in his rookie season. More NFL offensive coordinators should seek to blend their rookie franchise quarterback's college offensive concepts into their pro ones.

* * *

Highly drafted rookie franchise quarterbacks who enter teams in high-pressure situations without much talent around them are even more susceptible to lasting damage. The David Carr experience alone exemplifies that. These are situations where it makes sense to sit the quarterback initially. As Carr emphasized, teams are often wasting their pick if they toss the rookie into such losing, punishing scenarios.

The design for the 2017 highly drafted class of Trubisky, Mahomes, and Watson is to sit, watch, and learn behind veteran quarterbacks. The team's early post-draft starting quarterback plans were that Mahomes will follow Alex Smith, Watson will follow Tom Savage/Brandon Weeden, and Trubisky will follow Mike Glennon, though only Smith among them has more than five years of NFL experience.

Of course, the Philadelphia Eagles talked a similar plan for Carson Wentz in 2016, too, before he started all 16 games.

"It depends on where you are as a franchise and how you acquire him," Wisenhunt said. "Today, if you are picked highly as a QB you have to play. I don't think sitting will become the norm again because these young franchise quarterbacks are high-profile and play the most important position on the field. It is a dynamic position. When I was in Tennessee in 2015 and we drafted Marcus Mariota, he was going to play early. And he handled it. There is no cookbook way. You have to spend time with these guys before the draft and after the draft and find out the things they can do and what they can handle.

"It's an easy thing to say about the coaching criticisms in the league today, but everybody does it differently. A lot of different ways to skin a cat in this league. And a lot of people believe if it's not their way, it's wrong. All I know is, as great as any coach is, you are talking about coaching some rookie quarterbacks from the base of them not knowing how to take a snap from center. Working from that starting point can be a struggle for any coach."

* * *

In today's NFL, a rookie franchise quarterback is drafted, usually attends a three-day minicamp soon afterward, and then is limited to specific, structured practices before training camp starts in late July. This goes for all NFL players under their 2011 collective bargaining agreement that runs through 2021. The three phases are strength/conditioning/rehab, on-field workouts (no live contact), and organized team activities, known as OTAs.

NFL OFFSEASON WORKOUT PROGRAM RULES
(via NFL's release)
Voluntary offseason workout programs are intended to provide training, teaching, and physical conditioning for players.

As per Article 21 of the Collective Bargaining Agreement, each club's official, voluntary nine-week offseason program is conducted in three phases:

- **Phase One** consists of the first two weeks of the program with activities limited to strength and conditioning and physical rehabilitation only.
- **Phase Two** consists of the next three weeks of the program. On-field workouts may include individual player instruction and drills as well as team practice conducted on a "separates" basis. No live contact or team offense vs. team defense drills are permitted.
- **Phase Three** consists of the next four weeks of the program. Teams may conduct a total of 10 days of organized team practice activity, or "OTAs." No live contact is permitted, but 7-on-7, 9-on-7, and 11-on-11 drills are permitted.

Article 22 of the Collective Bargaining Agreement stipulates that clubs may hold one mandatory minicamp for veteran players. This minicamp must occur during Phase Three of the offseason program.

New head coaches are entitled to conduct an additional voluntary veteran minicamp. Any voluntary minicamp for veteran players must be conducted prior to the NFL Draft (April 27–29), but no earlier than week three of the club's offseason workout program and after at least one week of the two weeks of Phase One activities that the clubs may hold pursuant to Article 21. This year, five clubs will hold voluntary veteran minicamps.

Each club may hold a rookie football development program for a period of seven weeks, which in 2017 may begin on May 15. During this period, no activities may be held on weekends, with the exception of one post-NFL Draft rookie minicamp, which may be conducted on either the first or second weekend following the draft. The dates of each club's post-draft rookie minicamps will be circulated at a later date.

Few coaches in or out of the league like it.

"It's killing the game," Martz said. "You don't have these young quarterbacks around as much in the offseason and it's killing it. There's no correlation to college football and the NFL now, and it's really harder to teach them. They need development. They need to work on footwork, on learning the craft. They went overboard with the CBA. We aren't developing the other skill players, the wide receivers and cornerbacks, in that way, too. Let these young skill players, not even the veterans, come in, with no hitting, no contact, and work on drops, drills, throws, footwork, film. It's a process to increase a player's skills way before you get to the field. The teams are sending these quarterbacks to people in cities where their young quarterbacks live to work with them during this time off. Most of these so-called quarterback gurus do not know what they are doing. They just run drills. There are some good ones out there, but not many."

Some NFL quarterbacks during this time off gather their receivers for their own passing drills. Dalton said he usually does it in early July in either Texas or California, and that it gives him a chance to build his own voice and relationship with his receivers.

He said people talk about "the other way, but I don't know what 'other' is." This is the CBA that has been in place since Dalton was a rookie.

Jon Gruden zinged: "Ten, fifteen, twenty years ago, you work with your players all damn day and get some reps in the offseason. The regulations now are the reality. So now they've got to use virtual reality instead of actually getting on the field? Are you kidding me? Quarterbacks are not being taught certain things. It's another reason you see these bubble screens and some read options in the NFL and the no-huddle and why you're seeing it on every level—high school, college, and the pros. There isn't the time. There isn't the repetition he needs to learn. So, you get a young guy, just play him. That's the only way he's going to get better. You play them."

Les Snead said it is simply too much offseason time off for all quarterbacks, especially rookies.

"Tom Brady didn't do it that way," Snead said. "Peyton Manning didn't and Aaron Rodgers didn't. But the CBA is the CBA. We're probably not solving that one for a while. But it is a reminder—everyone is not custom built."

* * *

Wade Phillips has been a shrewd defensive expert in the NFL since 1976 with the then Houston Oilers. He has spent much of his NFL career as a head coach or defensive coordinator.

He will be joining the Los Angeles Rams for the 2017 season as their defensive coordinator.

During his extensive career, he has seen a heap of rookie quarterbacks.

"The key with a rookie is if he is made of the stuff where failing will not kill him," Phillips said. "Peyton Manning led the league in interceptions his first year and won three games. But the key was he didn't take sacks and he didn't take a ton of hits.[4] He was resilient and he wasn't letting the adversity kill his spirit. You can throw them in there but you have to keep the expectations not too high. Pick a goal you are trying to accomplish. When Doug Flutie was with the Bears, they threw him in there and he got eaten up. Then he went to Canada and set nearly every passing record up there. I have no doubt he would have been just as good in the NFL if he had time to develop early. Know your quarterback."

Phillips was the defensive coordinator in Philadelphia in 1986, and saw then head coach Buddy Ryan begin to play starter Ron Jaworski on first and second downs and then bring in young Randall Cunningham on third downs. It was a creative way, Phillips said, of getting Cunningham work and acclimated.

He said the most impressive rookie quarterbacks he has faced during his coaching career are Warren Moon (1984) when he first entered the league from the CFL, Peyton Manning (1998), and Michael Vick (2001).

Phillips along with Bill Belichick are routinely regarded as NFL defensive specialists who give rookie quarterbacks terror and horror in frustrating initial matchups. Both often make rookie quarterbacks look completely spooked.[5]

---

4. Of the 18 rookie quarterbacks to have started all 16 games, Manning's 22 sacks were the second-lowest of all time. (Matt Ryan was sacked only 17 times in his rookie season, 2008, with the Atlanta Falcons.)

5. Since 2000, rookie starting quarterbacks are 5–19 against the New England Patriots, with 21 touchdowns and 32 interceptions. They average around 185 yards a game and a quarterback rating of 64.7.

Phillips has learned to lock in on the one specific element that hounds rookie quarterbacks playing in their first few NFL games.

"Different looks," Phillips said. "You give that rookie quarterback something different from what they are used to seeing and have been seeing. That usually throws them off a bit. They don't know sometimes how to react to it. They have been coached so much on things like, 'If this is there, look for this.' You throw them off that type of coaching with a lot of surprises."

Phillips said he learned critical quarterback lessons long ago.

He is a defensive architect at heart, but passes the baton to finding and grooming a rookie franchise quarterback as the single most important thing for a head coach. He considers it the paramount task for a team and for a franchise to resolve.

"It's going like it's going now, and it won't change much," Phillips said. "People realize, the quarterback is key. You can play great defense and all that stuff, but you got to have a quarterback to win. Some teams draft one every year it seems. And there is something to that. You can trade up and pay a high price, you can get lucky in the later rounds, but you have to keep doing it, keep trying. They say defense wins championships, but not very many win without a quarterback. He is the guy that controls the game for you, scores points, has the ball in his hands the last two minutes to win it. It happens with defense, but it is hard to win it all with just defense. I know."

So does the NFL.

The 2018 draft is already predicted to yield three quarterbacks in the first three picks: USC's Sam Darnold, UCLA's Josh Rosen, and Wyoming's Josh Allen. That has not happened in the NFL since 1999, when Tim Couch, Donovan McNabb, and Akili Smith were consecutively chosen at the top.[6]

For the NFL, this apparently cannot happen enough. A larger pool. A more elite one right at the top.

Another swing for a rookie franchise quarterback. And the pressure, the temptation, the gamble to start him as he walks through the door.

* * *

Why do NFL teams gamble on starting rookie quarterbacks?

Well, NFL teams are in it to win a Super Bowl. Actually, to win multiple Super Bowls. Sometimes this gets lost with all of the intricate and fancy particulars and offshoots of the game. But the successful owners, the prize coaches, the prominent franchises in the league focus everything on one goal: we are in this to become champions.

A team cannot win it every year. None has. Few have won more than one championship. Fewer have won back-to-back championships. All want it. Some want it more. Some are smarter about how to claim it.

It starts with securing a franchise quarterback.

This is not to diminish the other pieces, the other important work, the exacting and eminent culture required for building a winning organization. But without a franchise quarterback, you are on a train on a track to nowhere.

---

6. Of those three quarterbacks, McNabb was the only one to have success in the NFL, being named to six Pro Bowls during his career.

Thus, this is why teams gamble on starting rookie quarterbacks. It is why they gamble on paying huge capital in various resources to obtain one.

But the tricky aspect remains that in most instances you just don't know what you have until after you have it. How do you reduce the risks? In an inexact exercise, how do you create a path to securing a franchise quarterback? As everyone associated with the NFL has described here, there are 32 different answers to that question representing 32 different teams. And plenty more from outside experts and influences. And millions more from invested fans.

We know that a trade for one is rare. If a team has one it is not eager to lose him.

The draft is the prevalent route. Some of it is just pure luck. How elite the crop of quarterbacks is coming out of college when an NFL team is in position to draft near the top is not something that it can control.

If you want to trade for the top pick but the team that owns it is in dire need of a franchise quarterback, you have little shot in prying that pick away. But if you want one badly enough, if you make the choice that there is a college quarterback you love, in some instances, if you pay big in current and future trade cache, you can get him.

What we also have learned is that drafting a franchise quarterback is a process that should be at least a year to three years in the making. A team must survey the college pool, identify a target, begin to get in position, and prepare to make its move.

This is what the Los Angeles Rams did in drafting Jared Goff. This is what the Philadelphia Eagles did in drafting Carson Wentz. This is what the Chicago Bears did in a shorter period, in a stealthy manner, plotting its move, making a firm decision, striking for Mitchell Trubisky.

Start him? Or sit him? Well, what other choice do you have? If you can play him without getting him killed, start him. Quarterbacks learn the game by playing. Trust your eyes, trust your ears once you get your hands on him in your own building and in your own practices. Is he on the fast track? Is he absorbing this offense at lightning speed? Can he play *now*? Is he already the best we have? Then start him.

Sit him if you have a plan—but have a plan. Either way, groom him effectively.

Quite clear in the process of grabbing a rookie franchise quarterback is that if his leadership and communication skills suffer, don't bother. Run. That guy cannot work. He cannot succeed. We have seen where ownership gets involved, falls in love, and forces a quarterback on a coach and a team. This is reckless and catastrophic to the process. It cannot be overcome.

When people talk about the head coach-quarterback relationship in the NFL, being more CEO-type now with clear divisions, clear lines of separation, limited in its communication frequency, and in its actual connections, that is alarming. It is not typically the best approach for success in today's NFL. It is not a conducive approach to today's young quarterbacks. Head coaches need to become more involved with these rookie quarterbacks, more selective in the offensive coordinators they choose to groom them. Too many careless mistakes are being made in those choices. Too many wrong fits. And, as previously discussed, too many voices in their ear from the head coach to the offensive coordinator to the quarterback coach to the passing game coach . . . reduce, simplify, centralize that.

How is it possible that teams missed the leadership and communication excellence of Dak Prescott? Maybe they didn't. Maybe his DUI so close to the draft process just pushed them away. Maybe they just didn't like the spread offensive elements he ran in college and graded him as a run-of-the-mill quarterback. But anyone who spent five minutes with this quarterback who is worth a morsel as a scout must have seen his colossal leadership and communication abilities. Every general manager in the league, every owner should demand that their personnel departments review everything they said and wrote about Dak Prescott and learn what they missed—and why. Because since he lasted until the fourth round in the 2016 draft, he was there for the team that did more effective vetting. Maybe even Dallas should think that through as well, since they waited four rounds to make it happen. But at least they made it happen. Prescott is showing Dallas and this league that he is not a flash. He is a quarterback who is going to move beyond his rookie year into a different level. Every team trying to figure out how to identify a franchise quarterback need look no further than every inch of detail of the Dak Prescott story.

All of these years later, the Houston Texans have a new franchise quarterback after doing their part in their inaugural season of destroying David Carr. The NFL has learned important lessons from his story. Get the rookie franchise quarterback a functioning offensive line. You cannot swing and miss on the offensive line. Then build the weapons around him and make sure the right people on your staff are in his ear. Get him a strong veteran example. Don't force it. If you are a lousy team, sit him if you must.

A team must have already decided that he has the intelligence, the DNA, the mentality, the processing to be its guy.

Because if you missed on that, you're stuck. Blow it up. Get him out. Start over. Swing again. This has been happening in recent NFL seasons; teams willing to part quickly with the "chosen" guy who quickly becomes the guy they can't boot fast enough. And that's OK. As long as they change the approach, open their minds on how to initially identify the right guy. As long as they are open to new approaches in testing and in having the right people in place to assess the quarterback's makeup, mentality and his ability to process in the classroom and on the field.

Put him in a quarterback room with care. Make that room special. Make sure he is around the right examples, the right reinforcements. Choose who is teaching him and what he is being taught from your coaching staff with the utmost weight.

Where is the NFL in this task? Where is it going? Some teams are set. Some have a hopeful franchise quarterback waiting. Some have little to nothing. Some have no clue.

But the question and the need remain. The task of identifying what a franchise quarterback looks like, what he talks like, how he works, and how you get one is an NFL constant. A huge need. It is a quest, a gamble where both should be managed and reduced.

Why do NFL teams gamble on starting rookie quarterbacks?

It is part of the puzzle of chasing the Super Bowl, part of a baffling, merciless championship mix that is so rough to reap.

AFTERWORD BY TONY DUNGY

The first shock wave of the 2017 NFL Draft came when the Chicago Bears traded three future picks to the San Francisco 49ers to move up one spot in the draft. Their reason for doing so was to make sure they were able to select the quarterback they coveted: University of North Carolina's Mitchell Trubisky. Despite having only started 13 games for the Tar Heels, the Bears were convinced he was their quarterback of the future. Trubisky immediately signed a four year, $29 million contract. This took place just after they had given free agent quarterback Mike Glennon a three-year, $45 million contract with over $18 million guaranteed.

In spite of all they gave up to acquire two unproven quarterbacks, it's hard to fault the Bears' thinking. In today's NFL it is so difficult to win without an elite quarterback that when you don't have one no price seems too high to pay. With the future of the Bears now resting in the hands of two inexperienced quarterbacks the $74 million question is, "How will they go about developing their franchise quarterback?"

That's really the question every franchise has to answer if they want to have a successful run at the top of the league. The teams who are consistently in the playoffs—New England, Pittsburgh, Indianapolis, Green Bay—have one thing in common: great quarterback play. I know what a difference that quarterback play can make. I was blessed to have one of the best who ever played the game in Peyton Manning. The Colts made the playoffs all seven of the years I coached there and won 12 or more games in six consecutive seasons. We had a lot of talented players, but there is no question having Peyton gave us the ability to be consistent winners.

So how do you find and, more importantly, how do you develop a franchise quarterback? What we've seen over the years is that there is no one, single way to do it. Peyton Manning was drafted No. 1 overall and immediately plugged into the starting lineup. He struggled through an interception-filled, 3–13 year but learned lessons that shaped a Hall of Fame career. Tom Brady was a 6th round draft choice who started his career backing up an established veteran in Drew Bledsoe (a former No. 1 overall pick). He was forced into the lineup by an injury to Bledsoe, but played with poise and confidence, leading the New England Patriots to the Super Bowl. Aaron Rodgers was a 1st round pick of the Green Bay Packers when they already had a future Hall of Famer in Brett Favre. Rodgers spent three years backing up Favre, but that was the Packers' plan all along. That plan resulted in Green Bay receiving over a quarter century of stellar quarterback play.

While there are different paths for young quarterbacks to take, there seem to be a few key elements to having them achieve success. First is a stable organization and system. The coaching staff may experience some changes but the system and the concepts need to remain the same. When I took over for Jim Mora after

Peyton Manning's fourth season, we kept Offensive Coordinator Tom Moore and the same offensive system. Manning would run that system his entire time in Indianapolis. I believe it is critical for a young quarterback to have the chance to grow in the same system, especially early in his career. It's not just a matter of learning your plays and your reads. There is so much for a young quarterback entering the NFL to learn about defenses and what opponents are doing. If you have to start over learning a new offense with new terminology and new reads it will slow down the developmental process. When you look at the top quarterbacks in the league today, most of them have benefitted from having stability from their coaching staffs.

Having a stable organization also allows you to sign and draft players who fit the QB's talents. As you learn your quarterback's strengths and weaknesses you begin to acquire players who compliment him. The young quarterback improves, not just because he is getting better, but because the talent around him improves as well. Peyton Manning would have found a way to be successful in the NFL under any circumstances, but playing in the same offensive system while the Colts brought in smart, versatile skill position players such as Edgerrin James, Reggie Wayne, Dallas Clark, and Brandon Stokley certainly made it easier for him to succeed.

The organization also has to do a great job in building the confidence of the quarterback. That's easy to do if it's a Ben Roethlisberger or Dak Prescott, who stepped into situations with very good offensive talent with veteran players. They were able to lead their teams into the playoffs, and confidence was never an issue. That situation, however, is not the norm. Most young quarterbacks are going to struggle their first couple of years.

Some don't play at all. It's up to the organization to have a plan of how to handle things if the quarterback doesn't have immediate success or if they make the decision not to play him early on. In this era of intense media coverage and social media scrutiny this is becoming even more important. While you can't control the reactions of media and fans, it is imperative that the team does a good job of keeping a positive attitude within the organization concerning the future of their quarterback.

As the 2017 season is set to unfold, we can rattle off a handful of teams we see as favorites to get to the Super Bowl because they have elite quarterbacks. For the others, their challenge is to find and develop a quarterback. How well they navigate that process will go a long way in determining the success of their franchise in the next decade. We will get a chance to see how the Bears plan unfolds and how well they answer their $74 million question.

It doesn't matter what team you root for, though. At some point there will come a time in the next couple of years when they will have to develop a young quarterback. As you watch your favorite team try to navigate this process I believe this book will help you look beneath the surface as you try to evaluate how well they're doing. It will help you understand some of the subtle factors that will determine if their young quarterback will develop into that elite, franchise quarterback that every team covets.

ACKNOWLEDGMENTS

Blitzed, this NFL historical and current analysis of identifying, grooming, and sometimes finger-crossed-praying for the emergence of franchise quarterbacks took several twists over the last year in research and interviews. Keen meaning was provoked when those conversations revealed the depth of quarterbacks' and teams' sorrow for the connections that failed and the lingering euphoria among those that thrived.

This subject is among the most critical, sensitive, humiliating, exhilarating, and consuming among NFL franchises and their fans. After being intricately involved with the NFL for nearly thirty years, *Blitzed* was my passion and honor to write.

Kind thanks to every NFL coach, every player, every owner and management source who contributed incessantly to this work. A special thanks to Jon Gruden and Tony Dungy, whose voices weave throughout this book in a distinctive, insightful way; men who had the most to say and said it in a manner that cannot be ignored for anyone seeking to solve the NFL franchise quarterback enigma. A salute to Mike Martz, for his courage and candor that induced illuminating thought to this subject. Warren Moon deserves particular acknowledgement for his piercing foreword that exemplifies the stellar way he approached quarterbacking en route to a Hall of Fame career.

Tremendous thanks to my SBNation team and to NFL editor Ryan Van Bibber, who have always inspired excellence. Particular gratitude to Jason Katzman, my editor at Sports Publishing, who was patient, diligent, and visionary. Additional thanks to the entire Sports Publishing crew.

Thank you to Leigh Steinberg for his class, integrity, and insight. Thanks to Joban for your support in this project. Sincere appreciation to Jewel and Pearl, constant reminders of the gift and joy of life.

To Tamara, Anthony, and Ely—great love and appreciation.

I am humbled by the measure of this work and everyone involved in it.

INDEX

Tannehill, Ryan, xvin1, 95
Tarkenton, Fran, 9n2
Tebow, Tim, 152
Tennessee Titans, xvii, xviin2, 22–23, 23n3, 25, 29–30, 45, 48, 51, 60, 100, 126, 135–38, 140, 155
Texas Christian University (TCU), 148–49
Texas Tech, 143
The Star, 83
Tittle, Y. A., xxi
Tomsula, Jim, xxiv,
Trubisky, Mitchell, xviii, 143, 154, 163, 167,
Tucker, Mel, xxiv,
Twitter, 151

U

United States Football League (USFL), 138, 147n1
University of California (Cal), 3, 20, 23, 26, 29–30, 105, 129
University of California-Los Angeles (UCLA), 160
University of Houston, 89
University of Memphis, 3
University of Michigan, 52
University of North Carolina, 143, 167
University of Oregon, 2
University of Southern California (USC), 100, 112, 160
University of Texas, 100, 135–37
University of Utah, 112

University of Wisconsin, 55, 57, 76
University of Wyoming, 160
USA Today, 76–77

V

Vermeil, Dick, xix, xxiii, 25–26, 48, 153
Vick, Michael, 122, 127, 159
Vinatieri, Adam, 109–10

W

Walsh, Bill, 35, 43, 104
Walter, Andrew, 95
Warner, Kurt, 20, 46–48, 104, 130, 133, 147
Washington Redskins, xxi, 1, 25, 35, 37, 44–45, 60, 70–71, 74, 81, 89, 92, 102–04, 148,
Washington State, 26
Watson, Deshaun, 96, 141–43, 152, 154
Wayne, Reggie, 169
Weary, Fred, 94n2
Webb, Davis, 14, 129–30
Weeden, Brandon, xxiv, 64n1, 97n3, 142, 154
Weinke, Chris, 105
Wentz, Carson, xviii, xxvi, 1–15, 17–18, 20, 22–23, 25, 30, 32, 36, 38, 44, 105–06, 154, 162
Whitworth, Andrew, 38
Williams, Doug, xviii, 44–45, 131–32, 134